THE LAST OF
THE CONFEDERATE PRIVATEERS

Captain John Clibbon Brain: Confederate States Navy (1865),
reproduced by courtesy of
United States Naval Records

THE LAST OF THE CONFEDERATE PRIVATEERS

DAVID and JOAN HAY

PAUL HARRIS PUBLISHING

EDINBURGH

First published 1977 by
Paul Harris Publishing
25 London Street
Edinburgh

ISBN 0 904505 23 5

Printed in Great Britain by The Scolar Press, Ilkley.

Contents

v

List of Illustrations

LIST OF MAPS

Acknowledgements

One of the most rewarding things about historical research is that one can write, out of the blue, to complete strangers who invariably take a great deal of trouble to help. Thus we are grateful to Les Bronson of the *London Free Press*, Ontario, for information about activity on Lake Erie—and incidentally to our old friend Silvia Clarke for putting us in touch with him.

I have always had a great admiration for Bruce Catton's histories and thank him for his kind permission to quote a few extracts.

We are grateful to F. Seal Coon of the *Gleaner and Star*, Kingston, Jamaica, and Clinton V. Black, Government Archivist for Jamaica, for material about the *St. Mary*'s. The Rev. J. M. B. Roberts of St. James, Clerkenwell, was very helpful about the location of his parish registers; Professor Lloyd suggested some background reading, and Mrs. Phillips of the United States Information Service and Miss Ziman of the United States Library, University of London, advised us about possible sources.

Our thanks go also to Mrs. Sandy Sims of the *Louisville Times*, Kentucky; William C. Davis, Editor of the *Civil War Times* of Harrisburg, Pennsylvania; Douglas L. Wilson, Director of the Knox College Library, Galesburg, Illinois; and J. C. Aldridge of the Public Record Office. For illustrations we are indebted to the Director of the West Point Military Academy Museum and the Commanding Officer, Naval Photographic Center, Washington D.C., and the National Maritime Museum, Greenwich.

We should add too our warmest thanks to Mr. C. Rippon, our County Librarian, and the staff of his Chesham branch for the endless trouble they have taken to obtain old and obscure books for us.

As usual the book is enhanced by the illustrations of our old friend Dennis Mallet and the excellent maps and harbour drawings of James Trotter.

Lastly, a book of this kind presupposes not only an interest in but also an affection for America itself, and its history. This cannot all be acquired from books alone and if it hadn't been for the kindly hospitality on many occasions over the last thirty years of my two charming cousins, Betty Kerr and Virginia Blandi, this book would probably not have been written.

Preamble

'Bold Captain Brain'

That night we found the steamer, the *Roanoke* by name,
Commanded by bold Captain Brain and all his gallant men,
Who took her from the Yankees, as she left the Cuban shore,
On the twenty-ninth September, in eighteen sixty-four.

So runs the second of sixteen verses of one of the many popular ballads about John Clibbon Brain that were circulating through the opera houses of the Southern States in that grim year just before final defeat and starvation. This one was printed at the office of the *Bermuda Mirror* in 1864 and sung to the tune 'Langford Gaol'.

Now, unless you are one of the growing number of people on both sides of the Atlantic who have become interested in the American Civil War—the first modern war, it has been called—or have relatives in the Southern States, I doubt if you will have heard of this rather unusual sailor. If he had not been one of my grandfather's less orthodox nephews, I might never have read his letters and been told about him by my Aunt Elizabeth. She knew him personally and was never quite sure whether he was a fit subject for conversation.

John Clibbon Brain, then about twenty years of age, arrived in the New World just in time for this war during which infant steam and the first ironclads burst unceremoniously into the world of sail and the old traditional ways. You can of course read the official account of his doings in the *History of the Confederate States' Navy* which was written by J. Thomas Scharf, A.M., LL.D., who was himself an officer in that service.[1] It covers the navy of the Southern States from its organisation to the 'surrender of its last vessel, its struggle with the great navy of the United States; the engagements fought in the rivers and harbors of the South, and upon the high seas; blockade-running, first use of ironclads and torpedoes and privateer history'.

But though you would get a brief, and in some respects inaccurate, summary of his main actions from this history, written twenty-two years after all records had been destroyed, I am afraid you would miss the whole flavour of this colourful and quite unclassifiable man. He doesn't fit into any of the historian's normal and well-worn pigeon holes. He spent almost as much time in gaol as in seizing enemy ships under the nose of the United States Navy. His private life may, in later years, have become something of a public scandal, and yet there is a sort of panache about all his doings that still comes to us very clearly across the intervening hundred years since the war ended. Indeed, even the end of the war does not seem to have put a damper on his activities. Afterwards we find him and his ex-crewmates happily running a circus, featuring wartime events, in order to earn bread and butter in an otherwise starving countryside. Of course, the Confederates were always the 'goodies' and the Northerners the 'baddies'.

The casual reader might be forgiven for writing him off as an adventurous young man with a gift for showmanship, who welcomed the war as a state of affairs in which simple piracy was elevated to the respectable realms of professional and authorised privateering, complete with a commission and the appropriate Letters of Marque. They would be just as wrong as the very human sailors who composed and sang rollicking, if ungrammatical and somewhat limping, ballads about him in the dockside taverns and opera houses of the Southern States. He may have been a bit of an opportunist, with perhaps a quicksilver temperament which included a truly feminine and objective concern for the present, uninhibited by any qualms about the future. He may not have had quite the same idealistic belief in the sanctity of the Southern States as some of his more serious-minded brother officers. But who among us is qualified to stand up and point the finger of scorn on that account? Besides, is not history the sum of human actions and the distillation of their results?

He must have had that indefinable something that men in a crisis will follow instinctively. His own men would have followed

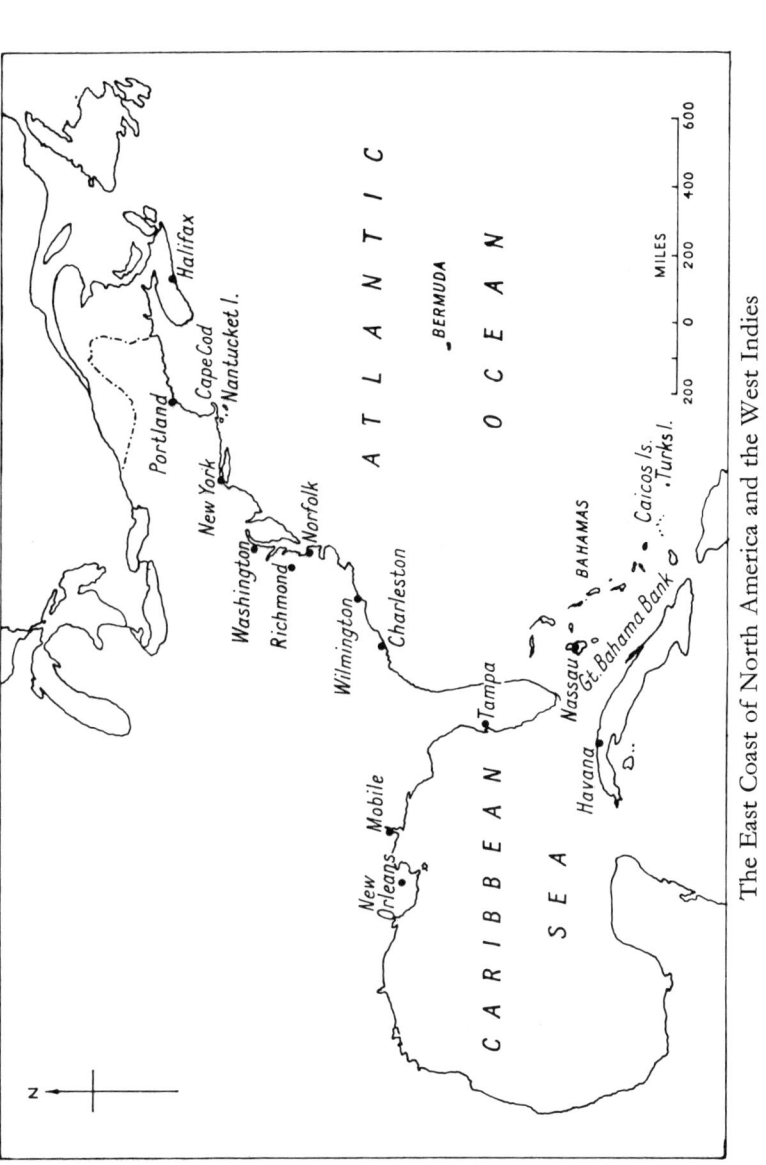

The East Coast of North America and the West Indies

him happily into the most alarming escapade—and frequently did so in the course of the war.

His mother, Eliza, was a Tabram, one of a family who were individualists if nothing else. One of them was to get, I think, as near as anyone to a verbal evaluation of Brain by saying, 'He alters like a clear pool to every mood of the sky so that the shallow observer might forget how deep the waters really are.'

So it is to the Tabram papers[2] and contemporary cuttings from American, British, and Canadian newspapers, as well as many official documents, that we must turn for the more human aspects of John Clibbon Brain, sometime master and acting commander in the navy of the Confederate States of America: a navy which did not exist before the war started and which was created out of nothing.

The Bannut Tree House

EARLY DAYS IN ENGLAND

This is not a book about Brain's early life in England, but about his part in the American Civil War. I think it would be as well, however, to mention some aspects of family background which must have coloured his outlook and certainly help to explain some of his later exploits. The head of the Tabram family at the time young Brain was born was his grandfather (and my great-grandfather), John Clibbon Tabram, who lived at the Bannut Tree House, Nailsworth, in Gloucestershire (illustration p. 9). This house, with its fourteenth-century chapel and the later additions to the priest's house which had been carried out in the fifteenth century, remained the old family home until a few years ago. It is here that master John Brain makes his first appearance in the family papers at the tender age of 2½ years. He had been brought down from London by his parents for his sister's christening.

As the Bannut Tree House meant a great deal to J. C. Brain in later life and indeed was regarded by him as home, it is worth having a closer look at the charming little gathering recorded in my great-grandfather's diary. He had got permission from the Bishop for the chapel to be used again as such for the ceremony, one of the three times that this had been allowed since it was deconsecrated, probably at the time of the Reformation. The old roof had collapsed and had been replaced by a fresh lot of great Cotswold cut stones, but the worst tragedy had been that the lovely old tiled floor of slipwear tiles from Keynsham Abbey had more or less disappeared and by this time there was a wooden floor again which enabled the chapel to serve as an office and savings bank, the first that the village had ever had. On this day, however, all the furniture had been cleared away and hastily piled into

Extract from the Tabram Family Tree
(To show John Clibbon Brain's relationship to those few mentioned in the book)

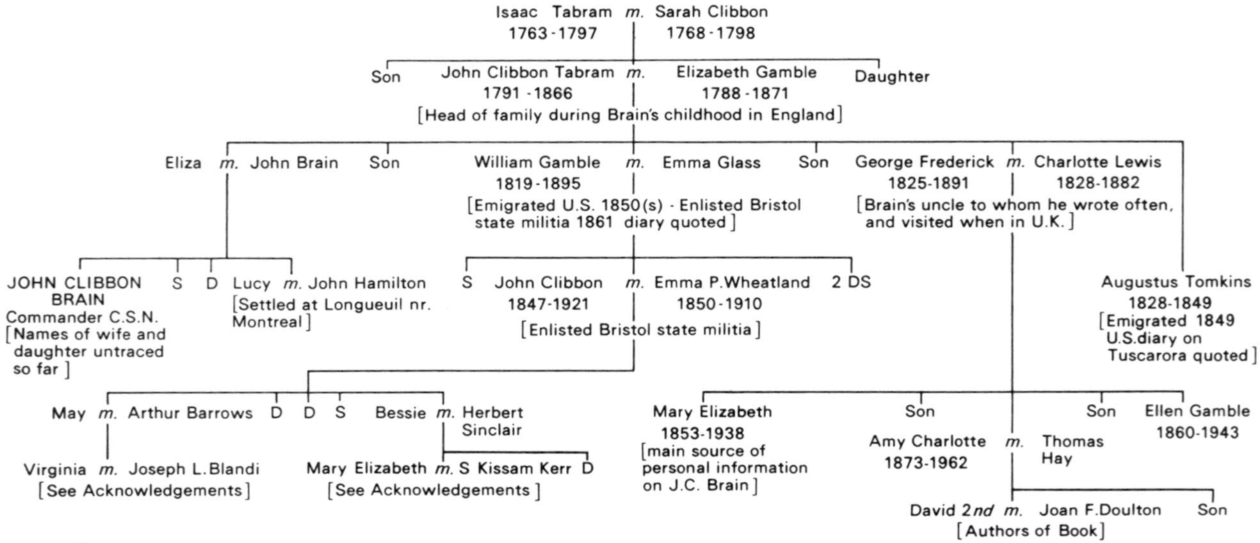

Isaac Tabram *m.* Sarah Clibbon
1763-1797   1768-1798

Son | John Clibbon Tabram *m.* Elizabeth Gamble | Daughter
1791-1866   1788-1871
[Head of family during Brain's childhood in England]

Eliza *m.* John Brain | Son | William Gamble *m.* Emma Glass | Son | George Frederick *m.* Charlotte Lewis | Augustus Tomkins
1819-1895   1825-1891   1828-1882   1828-1849
[Emigrated U.S. 1850(s) - Enlisted Bristol state militia 1861 diary quoted]
[Brain's uncle to whom he wrote often, and visited when in U.K.]
[Emigrated 1849 U.S.diary on Tuscarora quoted]

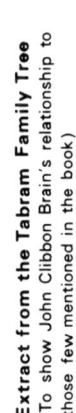

JOHN CLIBBON BRAIN S
Commander C.S.N.
[Names of wife and daughter untraced so far]

D Lucy *m.* John Hamilton [Settled at Longueuil nr. Montreal]

S John Clibbon *m.* Emma P.Wheatland | 2 DS
1847-1921   1850-1910
[Enlisted Bristol state militia]

Mary Elizabeth
1853-1938
[main source of personal information on J.C. Brain]

Son | Amy Charlotte *m.* Thomas Hay | Son Ellen Gamble
1873-1962   1860-1943

May *m.* Arthur Barrows | D | D | S | Bessie *m.* Herbert Sinclair | Mary Elizabeth *m.* S Kissam Kerr D | David 2nd *m.* Joan F.Doulton | Son

Virginia *m.* Joseph L. Blandi [See Acknowledgements]

Mary Elizabeth [See Acknowledgements]

David 2nd *m.* Joan F.Doulton [Authors of Book]

Legend
S = Son
D = Daughter
U.S.= United States

Extract from the Tabram family tree

the vestry and J. C. Tabram, who was something of a historian in his own right, must have had a lot of fun putting the whole place back to the days when there had been a resident priest and the people of Nailsworth had worshipped there instead of having to cover the two miles to the mother church at Avening. The chapel had, indeed, been a Chapel of Ease to Avening before the new church had been built. The main east window looked over the little valley and in the vestry, I remember, some child had made an enchanting design of sea shells set in plaster round the little piscina.

J. C. Tabram would have come down the old, well-worn stone newel staircase from the upper floors of the priest's house to the large kitchen and thence on to the lawn where his guests would be. The lawn, encircled by its carriage drive, was set against the chapel on one side and the long rambling house with its three-feet-thick stone walls on the other. I remember it so well from Christmas house parties when I was a child. At the far end of the garden rose the great bannut (walnut) tree from which the house had always taken its name, and down through the orchard he could probably see a small boy hand-in-hand with Uncle Fred, his favourite uncle. Uncle Fred was J.C.'s second son, and fortunately for us Brain seems to have been very fond of him because it is from the letters during the war to this uncle that we get much of our information. This day, according to the diary, they had both gone down to the orchard and were observing the age-old custom of telling the bees 'that his little sister had just been christened'. His Uncle Fred was explaining to him why all the hives had different colours and this, he said, was so that the bees should know their own homes—an odd family tradition kept up, I remember, till long after the turn of the century.

The whole scene must have looked very gay, and there are one or two photographs of the garden about this time, in the very early days of photography. There were the great family silver teapots and the tables set up with their embroidered cloths and the distinctive red-and-white-striped lustre tea service—most of which has fortunately survived that and later ceremonies. It was a set that all the young Tabrams were allowed to see and look at on special occasions along with the salt-glaze bear whose head revolved on his shoulders to alter the expression. This particular teaset had Biblical scenes of the most lurid nature, especially, one remembers, Moses, a rather large, substantial Moses lying on a minute cloud that looked as if it were about to let him down at any moment.[3] Each member of the family had his favourite cup.

Now there is nothing particularly distinguished or remarkable about the Tabram family except possibly the prominent nose which we all have in common and which seems to run right through both the English and American branches without exception. As you will see from his photograph (frontispiece), J. C. Brain certainly had it too. The Tabrams have always had a somewhat odd mixture of determination and artistic irrelevance. If the latter was the stronger then there were apt to be certain waywardnesses of temperament; if the former was predominant it created a strength of character which made a certain close friend once remark that there was not room for more than one Tabram in a house at the same time.

All the same, it was this ordinary, independent middle-class which kept the country stable no matter which way the Government of the day was trying to push it. Great-grandfather seems to have turned his hand to practically everything, from running a bank to auctioneering, registering births, and being more or less the centre of the little community of Nailsworth. One of his more delightful offices was treasurer for the Society for the Prosecution of Criminals. What they did or what it was in aid of, history doesn't relate, and the imagination boggles.

Elizabeth, J. C. Brain's mother, was J. C. Tabram's eldest child, with all the Tabram vitality bottled up by long habit and a straight-laced, conventional upbringing at the Bannut Tree, surrounded by maids in black dresses, starched caps and aprons, and the general aura of Sunday sanctity and weekday well-being. She certainly had no sympathy with other members of the family who were not quite as orthodox as they might have been. Brother Albin is described in one of her letters as 'pretending to be married but this is not so'. She didn't quite approve of her three nieces—John Clibbon Brain's first cousins—one of whom was my own mother.

It must have been from this side of the family that J. C. Brain

The Bannut Tree House, Nailsworth (Brain's family home on his mother's side)

got his stubbornness, his initiative, and his ability to bring dangerous project to a successful conclusion.

On the other hand, his father, John Brain, could hardly have
been more different and I imagine he must have felt ill at ease in
the comfortable, stuffy atmosphere of Bannut Tree House. Artistic
by his own assessment and lazy by nature, he tended always to
take the easy way out of his problems and the result was a precari-
ous, bohemian wandering existence which his wife must have
found hard to endure. The Brains lived in London and he had
tried hard to make a living as an artist, with very little success.
The vicissitudes in his career are indicated by the varying entries
in the parish register of St. James, Clerkenwell, where most of
their children were christened. Appearing at different times as
'Clerk' and 'Gent'—which I take to be a polite term for unemployed—he made his living mainly as a copper plate dealer and
engraver, but he seems to have engraved the wrong things and
went bankrupt in 1845, owing his father-in-law £1,050 which was
quite a large sum of money in those days.

The whole family life must have had its effect on the young boy
because his parents were always short of money, always having to
move house, sometimes in rather a hurry, and it can never have
been very clear where the next week's food was coming from. It
is not surprising that, with these widely differing parents, John
Clibbon Brain should have been rather a mixture. His antecedents
obviously go a long way towards accounting for his own split
personality, and perhaps we can see why his wartime and post-
war life was such a mixture of energetic achievement and apparent
inability to make anything of his life, without the stimulus of a
war. The only person (who had known and seen him in the flesh)
that I was able to talk to over a period of fifteen years or more in
later life was my Aunt Elizabeth. She was indeed hardly a teenager
at the time of the Civil War and I think disapproved of a considerable number of Brain's doings, but in later life, I could not help
feeling even her stern Victorian heart had a soft spot for this
wayward but affectionate boy.

Whenever things became too bad, Elizabeth Brain obviously
appealed to her father for help; but with her eldest brother
William Gamble Tabram also frequently in need of money J. C. T.

must have got a little desperate. There is a rather pathetic note in his Will, explaining why he had left everything to my grandfather: 'My son William Gamble Tabram and my daughter Elizabeth Brain having had large sums of money from me at various times, which I consider more than equivalent to what I now leave to my second son George Frederick . . .'.

So, it is hardly surprising to find that they took the only step which then seemed open to those who failed to solve the problem of living: they emigrated. Thus it was that both families went off to America and I suspect father Tabram was somewhat relieved to see them go. Fortunately the emigration does not seem to have made any sort of permanent rift in the family because the American branches still feature in the letters of John Clibbon Tabram, and young J. C. Brain himself went on writing to my grandfather, George Frederick. Otherwise we would have known very little about his activities, nor would the press cuttings have been collected and sent across to England.

2

'The Federal Flag at the Peak and the Confederate Flag at the Fore'

THE SOUTH FINDS ITSELF AT WAR

Emigrants like the Brain family arriving in New York in the late 1850s found themselves in a strange world—a world holding its breath for the big bang everybody secretly feared and openly scoffed at. A few politicians may have thought they knew what was going to happen, but certainly neither side expected there would be an actual war. To the mass of the population there seemed to be an uneasy balance between rumours of momentous events in high places and the calm of everyday life around them which seemed unaffected by such events altogether—at least in the South.

For the moment, however, the Brain family would have been more concerned with settling down in the New World and making a living than with local politics, and in this the feckless father, John Brain, seems to have been no more successful than he had been in England. He made his way west as far as Ohio, where he left his wife and disappeared for good, leaving her to bring up the family as best she could. His eldest son, John Clibbon, had inherited some of his father's artistic ability and had been taught the elements of the printing and engraving trades, but he obviously decided rapidly that the chances of making a satisfactory living at those trades were negligible and that he must find alternative ways of making his fortune.

The methods he chose were not exactly orthodox, and it is hardly surprising to find that the family papers contain no news of this stage of his life. Indeed, we should probably have heard nothing about his activities if he had not later achieved sufficient notoriety to get the newspaper reporters delving into his past.

'Who is Lieutenant Brain?' asked the *New York Times* on 31 October 1864, and the ensuing article starts with a lurid paragraph:

This reckless young scoundrel, was, just before the breaking out of the Rebellion, a lounger. His first venture, so far as is known, was in Williamsburg, Long Island, where he became acquainted with a young woman of low but respectable connections whom he eventually made his wife.

In reading this article one has to remember that there was in those days, especially during a vicious civil war, no such thing as impartial reporting. As the *New York Times* itself stated the next day, there were 'No neutrals in this war—only Patriots or Traitors'. The reporter had obviously been told to blacken the name of a Confederate naval privateer who had by then (1864) become a very real thorn in the side of the Northern States; but from the curious mixture of juvenile invective and muddled facts one thing does emerge—that Brain and his wife were fairly heavily in debt and wanted by the authorities for non-payment of hotel bills on a honeymoon which seems to have extended right across from the east to the west coast. Not a very auspicious start for a new boy in a New World!

By the time they reached 'the extreme point West', as the article says, the young couple were finding it difficult to know what to use for money and, you will not be surprised to learn, 'the young wife returned to Williamsburg, to the astonishment of the neighbours'. Eventually she received a note from Brain, only to return, a few months later, complete with an obviously new wardrobe and what the *New York Times* describes as 'a handbag full of gold'!

Well, well, your guess is as good as mine, but it is hardly surprising to find that Brain moved discreetly to the South where he may have felt that most people were too busy seceding from the Union to bother too much with a character who wanted to disappear for a time. The fact that he was a wanted man in the North may have been considered to his credit.

This book is not concerned with the reasons for the American

Civil War. However, if the naval manoeuvres in general and the doings of individuals in particular are to have any accurate historical location and significance, it is at least necessary to sketch in an outline of the background against which they were performed.

The Southern States did not expect secession to lead to war. After all, they had entered the Union voluntarily, so why should they not leave it again if it no longer suited them—particularly if t was trying to impose an unpalatable way of life upon them? I think that we in England are still inclined to forget how much power even today is vested in individual states. They control the whole of their own taxation and many elements of their basic way of life. Only for war and foreign policy do they combine under a federal flag. In those days, a hundred years ago, the scales were even more heavily weighted against central authority.

Secondly, it is perhaps worth recalling that there was really no single act of secession and, initially, no joint organisation of the seceding states. South Carolina set the ball rolling on 10 December 1860; this was followed by Mississippi, Florida, and Alabama on three consecutive days from 9 to 11 January 1861, and by Georgia on 18th, Louisiana on 26th, and Texas on 1 February. It was not till 4 February that the first meeting of the Southern States, as such, took place. After electing Jefferson Davis provisional President (see opposite) one of the first things the assembly did was to confirm all existing laws except those few which were in direct conflict with their own objects.

There was a delightful atmosphere of unreality about the whole affair. The population was busy reading world-shaking headlines in the papers, without being able to notice the slightest change in their own humdrum struggle for existence, or the boundless opportunities for pleasure among the rich planters. There seemed no prospect of this coming to an end. Any seafaring man must have been enchanted to notice that the steamers plying between New York and Savannah, quite oblivious of all the posturing and warlike noises ashore, were happily continuing to run until 4 April 1861, 'carrying the Federal flag at the peak and the Confederate flag at the fore'. They didn't even bother to change flags half-way, as today we might change courtesy flags when cruising

President Jefferson Davis—a contemporary photograph
sent home by Brain

out of one country's territorial waters into another's. One country
had become two so they just bought another flag to make everybody happy.

But tensions were rapidly building up, especially for the individual officer or trooper in the armed forces. They suddenly had to
work out whether their allegiance was primarily to the Union
Government and the service in which they had enlisted, or to
their own state, if they had come from the South. Some, like
Captain Buchanan, were so undecided that they resigned their
commissions and then only a fortnight later asked for reinstate-

ment. This was refused, so Captain Buchanan became one of the senior captains on the Confederate side.

On the whole, most of the officers who came from the Southern States felt that their duty lay with their countrymen and with the South rather than with the head of an armed force which might be turned against their home state. But it was, as Captain John Wilkinson,[4] later to be prominent in the Confederate States Navy, said, 'a painful act to separate themselves from companions with whom they had been long and intimately associated and from the flag under which they had been proud to serve'. I think probably this dilemma was worst for naval officers who, as Admiral Semmes[5] put it,

> had been rocked together in the same storm, and had escaped perhaps from the same shipwreck. West Point and Annapolis were powerful bonds to knit together the hearts of young men. Friendships were formed there, which it was difficult to sever, especially when strengthened by years of after association in common toils, common pleasures and common dangers.

By April 1861 the uneasiness and uncertainty as to whether the world was going to burst into flames or not can have been nowhere stronger and more in evidence than in the state of Virginia, where J. C. Brain seems to have taken refuge. A glance at the map will show the strategic importance of this state, controlling the southern and western shores of Chesapeake Bay and a potential threat to the capital from which it was only separated by the Potomac River. Worse still, however, was the location in this state of one of the most vital national assets, the Norfolk Navy Base and the ships inside it.

Virginia itself kept both sides on tenterhooks for two months while it seemed to be trying to tear itself in two in the struggle. At the beginning of April it had still voted against secession, despite its obvious sympathy with the Southern way of life. Then on 15 April President Lincoln issued a proclamation asking for 75,000 troops from each state. This was more than the Virginians could take and two days later they decided to join the South.

During the preceding week excitement had been mounting

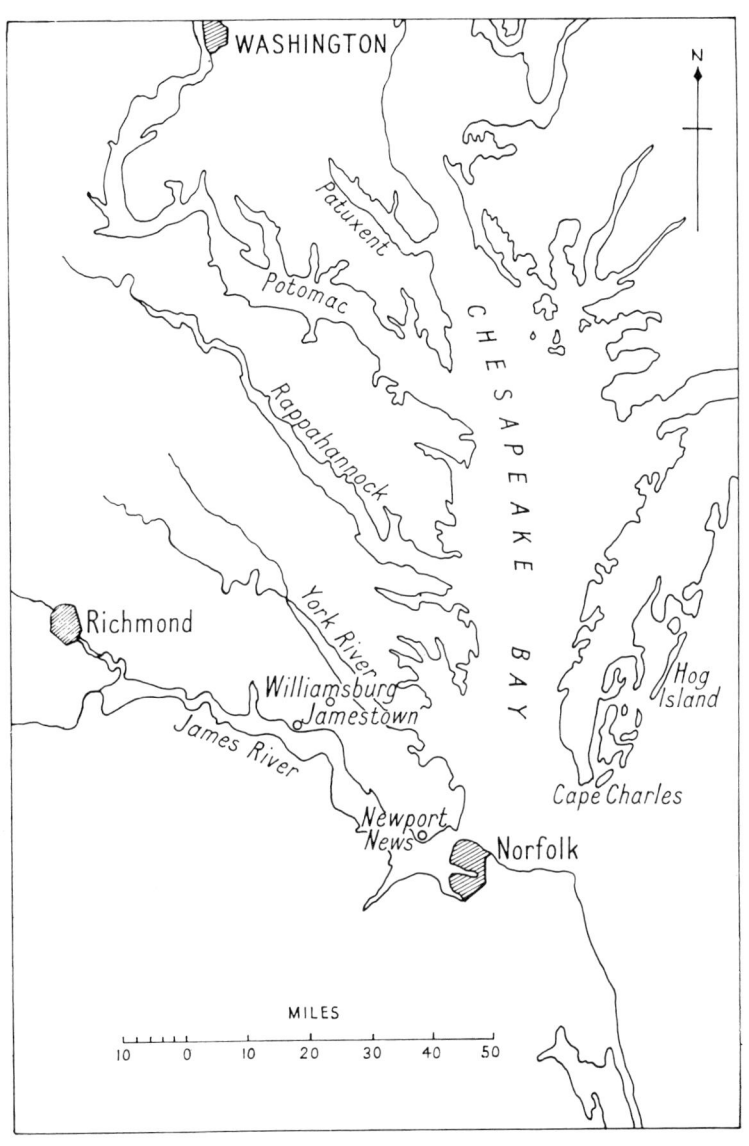

Chesapeake Bay with the Patuxent, Potomac, Rapphannock, York and James Rivers

around the Navy Base, for the dilemma for the Federal Government was obvious. To reinforce the base might antagonise the Virginians and drive them into the wrong camp; to leave it inadequately protected might amount to handing it over to the South if Virginia decided after all on secession.

It was not only Washington's dilemma. It was also a problem for the Commandant, Commodore Charles S. McCauley, a naval officer of fifty years' service and already sixty-eight years old. He was thought to be loyal to the Union, but most of the officers on his staff were of Southern descent and could quite fairly complain to an emissary from the Navy Board that they were 'painfully situated', particularly when the workers round them made no secret of their strong Southern sympathies. Back in Washington the navy was urging the army to send troops to protect the yard; the army, on the other hand, suggested that the navy should just sail the ships away, as being a much easier answer. The trouble was, as the navy pointed out, that some of the ships, and particularly the most important of them, the steam frigate *Merrimac* of 40 guns, were not ready for sea. McCauley seemed unwilling to set about preparing her and Washington had to send an engineer to work on her engines, and a senior officer, Commander James Alden, to take command before McCauley, in a dilatory sort of way, gave orders to make the ships ready for sea. After about four days' work the *Merrimac*'s engines were turning over and by 18 April she had steam up, but McCauley, who seemed 'stupefied, bewildered, and wholly unable to act', still would not let her go. In despair, Alden and his engineer Isherwood went back to Washington to report. It was too late. Virginia had signed the Act of Secession on 17 April.

Wild rumours were soon flying about. There were stories that the channel below Norfolk had been blocked, and a few masts had been seen sticking out of the water to prove it. The blockage was quite ineffectual, and the *Pawnee*, as we shall see, sailed past quite happily two days later. McCauley began to feel that he was becoming hemmed in in a hostile country of Southern sympathisers. To add to his discomfiture, there were rumours of Virginian troop movements. Indeed, General Taliaferra did arrive with two very small companies. In case this was not sufficient to make up the Commandant's mind, stories of the coming of three to five thousand troops were put about on the initiative of the president of the Norfolk and Petersburg railroad, who then proceeded to run empty cars a few miles up the railroad and return with them full of shouting citizens to create an impression of large reinforcements. There were further reports of a battery having been set up to command the fort. Some said guns were visible from the cross-trees of the *Cumberland* lying in the river.

All this was too much for poor McCauley. Just as the *Pawnee*, with Commodore Paulding aboard bearing orders to relieve him, was steaming round the block ships, Commodore McCauley suddenly leapt into action and ordered the ships to be scuttled. He added further that their guns were to be spiked. The *Pawnee* sailed past the cheering crew of the *Cumberland* to find the ship she had come to save already sinking and further rumours of great assemblies of people preparing to take the Navy Yard. An hour or two after his arrival, Paulding ordered the destruction of the yard, and by dawn he was on his way back down the river with the few ships which were still afloat. Meanwhile the result of his visit could be seen for miles up and down the estuary by the excited crowds. Fires were still burning in the naval yard as the last ships passed out, but though the ships had now gone, th demolition of the yard itself had been only partially successfu and it was found, as soon as the Southern sympathisers broke through, that much of the yard remained. This was a most valuable acquisition by the Confederate forces who had no naval bases of their own, no mills or industrial areas for manufacturing ships' parts, guns, or armaments of any sort.

This, then, was the topsy-turvy, but rather stimulating, world in which we hear of friend Brain volunteering for service in the army of the Confederate States.

3

'Come On, You Damned Volunteers'

THE FIRST MODERN WAR EVOLVES

By now war was inevitable and both sides were enlisting volunteers. For most individuals there was none of the heart-searching
that the serving officers had undergone. If you came from the
North you were a Unionist; if from the South you supported the
Confederacy. So we find William Gamble Tabram, Brain's uncle,
who had built up a flourishing ironmongery and general store in
Bristol, Pennsylvania, volunteering, with his seventeen-year-old
son, John Clibbon Tabram the second, for the Bristol State
Militia.

It is from him that we get the flavour of life as a volunteer in
those early days. It was by no means all beer and skittles, as
nothing was then organised. The few regular officers recalled to
duty were out of practice and imbued with the harsh disciplinary
methods of earlier times. The new officers who had bought their
commissions with money or influence had no more idea of how
to run camps than the troops themselves. In fact there was criti-
cism from both levels. Officers fulminated about wealthy private
soldiers, and the soldiers complained of their officers. But let
William Tabram tell his own story in a letter from Hagerstown,
twenty miles from the Potomac river and twenty-one from Bristol.

Dear Father and Mother,
    You will be surprised to hear from me. I am at last become a
soldier and am first corporal. But I must first tell you how I
came so, in as few lines as possible, as I am lying in my tent on
my belly writing this. In my last letter I spoke of the draft and
since I wrote the governor of the state found that the Southern-
ers were in Maryland and the state of Pennsylvania was in
danger of being invaded by them. . . .

John Clibbon Tabram, aged 17, as a volunteer in the
Bristol State Militia

We have in our company two Senators, one clergyman, two lawyers, one doctor, one man with $100,000 and another with $50,000 and many others. . . . The worst is the sleeping—a blanket around us, knapsack for pillow and sky above. We are on the move and used the railroad part of the way. The night before last we marched 15 miles after 7 o'clock at night and it was 3 in the morning before we camped but I had a tent and I had a fair sleep in a barn. We had 4,000 on our march. I belong to the 17th Pennsylvania Regiment (we muster a 1,000). We are about 7 miles from the battle ground. I can hear the cannons plainly. We are camped on a ground that the rebels occupied five days ago. Last night the rebel picket was within two miles of us but today they have retreated. I and the three men under me were put in charge of the prisoners. I can tell you we all felt uneasy. The rest of us slept with loaded muskets under us. I can't begin to tell you all the scenes I have witnessed. Within about three miles all round here we have about forty to fifty thousand soldiers of Pennsylvania brigades. The sight was amusing to one who has not witnessed the life before but what devastation and destruction of property.

J. C. Brain meanwhile had enlisted in the South and was being trained as a gunner. For all the dreary routine of battery duty at a station somewhere on the James River, life sometimes had its lighter moments as we gather from another contemporary account:

The battery at Acquia Creek was constructed as a terminus for the railroad from Friedricksberg and was manned by an infantry company acting as artillerists. Besides this force, permanently stationed at the battery and quartered near it, a company of infantry from military headquarters was sent every evening to guard against night attack. A company called the 'Tigers' took their turn at this service and we would gladly have dispensed with their 'protection'. Utterly undisciplined, they were more dangerous to friends than to foes. Mutinous and insubordinate, they were engaged in constant collisions with each other and with the company so unfortunate as to be quartered near them; their camp was a pandemonium. In addition to other sources of quarrel and contention several women (*vivandières* they called themselves) follow the company. The patience of General Meers who commands the division was finally exhausted. He summoned the Captain of the 'Tigers' into his presence; and after severely reprimanding him for the misconduct of his men, insisted that the *vivandières* should be sent away. The captain urged many reasons for keeping them; the chief one being the good 'moral effect' of their presence! But the general was inflexible. Even gallantry to the sex must be sacrificed to the truth; and a reformation commenced with the departure of the women; and our friends the 'Tigers' eventually became well-behaved soldiers.

Now, I do not suggest that there is any actual evidence to connect the 'Tigers' with our John Clibbon Brain but there is a very familiar ring about it, and it is the sort of company he would have enlisted in, given half a chance.

Perhaps the attitude of the few professional soldiers can best be found in the words of General Charles F. Smith—shouted over his shoulder as he led a division of pea-green troops up a hill under heavy fire to attack a Confederate position: 'Come on, you damned volunteers, now's your chance—you volunteered to be killed for love of country, now you can do it—I'm only a soldier and I don't damn well want to be killed.'

It must be remembered that the South soon found itself fighting a total war to avoid extinction. There were no holds barred. The old rules of civilised warfare were soon to disappear, and it became a case of hitting the enemy wherever you could find him and with whatever you could lay your hands on. In the early days the South had virtually no means of manufacturing weapons of its own. But for guns dredged up from the Norfolk Base it would have started the war virtually without any possibility of mounting batteries anywhere or of arming its few ships.

The South produced a lot of cotton but couldn't eat it and as soon as the Federal armies got going they were instructed to burn and destroy all crops and foodstuffs in any conquered Confederate states. The North, being rich, could afford a system of payment in lieu of call-up or the hiring of substitutes. Out of 85,000 drafted in New York in one year only 9,000 reached the firing line. In the South, the position was catastrophically reversed, as summed up by a recruit from South Georgia speaking of the medical examination: 'The army don't examine your eyes, it just counts 'em.'

In spite of the savagery which developed later—over half a million out of a total population of thirty million were killed, 360,000 in the North and 260,000 in the much smaller South (about one-fifth of the productive male population), while the maimed were never counted—it was a war of amateurs, amateurs like J. C. Brain who wandered in and fought under generals who had never heard a shot fired except at a game bird. At the battle of Shiloh where two completely green armies ran into each other head-on and fought non-stop for two days, a Middle-West corporal walking along the front line was heard explaining to his men, 'Don't get worried—it's just like shootin' squirrels—only these squirrels have got guns—that's all.'

I think the flavour possibly comes out best in the account (by Bruce Catton) of a New York regiment toiling at drill on a dusty hot field until a private turned to his captain and said, 'Say, Tom, let's quit this darn foolin' around and go see the Sutlers!'

It is with the navy, however, that we are concerned here, for it did not take J. C. Brain long to decide that battery duty was not to his liking, and that the navy might provide far more scope for adventure and amusement if he played his cards right. It was not difficult to arrange a transfer as there was a desperate shortage of crews. Indeed, sailors were obtained only by drafting in army personnel and training them from scratch on any available ship. So, as his infrequent letters to his Uncle Fred at the Bannut Tree House confirm, we find him posted to the *Jamestown* in the James River squadron for training as an able seaman. Thus began his career in the Confederate Navy, in which he became a substantive Master and Acting Commander.

Despite all the amateurism, the navy that Brain had joined was about to take part in the first modern war, with the first clash of ironclads, and the use of torpedoes and submarines (though these last were steam-driven and could not submerge entirely because the top of the funnel had to remain above water). Brain still spoke of his infantry weapon as a musket, meaning a muzzle-loading smooth bore, and yet by this time practically all sailors and infantrymen were carrying rifles. They were still muzzle loaders, but very different from the Brown Bess of tradition from which you were fairly safe at a distance of 150 yards—I think it was General Grant who remarked that 'a man might shoot at you all day from that distance without your being aware he was doing it'.

Enemy ships were now subject to sniping attack from rifle muskets a quarter or half a mile away, and the rifled guns were beginning to mean that fairly accurate gunnery could be counted upon up to several miles. As we know, it was not to be long before the target fired at was still below the horizon.

In order to counteract this new development one or two things had to be done rather hastily. Ever since the Greeks put armour on infantrymen to counter the attack of the Scythian horse bow-men, war has been a swing of the pendulum back and forth between the predominance of offensive weapons and the effective-ness of defensive armour. At the opening of the American Civil War the offensive weapons still held sway. But their effectiveness was to receive a sharp setback from the defence. First of all, boiler plates were hung around ships so that they could get close to their objective without suffering any real damage. No sooner was this accomplished than, in order to overcome these rather rudimentary armoured ships which could not be damaged by ordinary gunfire, the so-called 'spar torpedo' was invented. Because there was at that time no mechanism sufficiently efficient to make a torpedo run under water at a calculated depth, they were carried on long poles from the bows of ships, and simply rammed against the sides of enemy ships and detonated. Later they were to be delivered by little steamships, which operated almost completely submerged, except for the funnel. These spar torpedoes were similarly driven bodily into the underwater hulls of warships, or just spattered about the estuaries like modern mines. Indeed, we would now call them mines, but these were the things referred to by Admiral Faragut in his famous remark, 'Push on immediately and damn the torpedoes.'

In the year 1862, all this was only a few months in the future but it might have been a hundred years away as far as the young men manning the James River squadron were concerned.

There were in addition certain new materials of war which became important for the first time, such as coal, with the change-over from sail to steam. Indeed coal was not only used by the steam boats but at Acquia Creek, where J. C. Brain probably was stationed for a short time, they were lucky enough to acquire a large quantity of coal which had been stored in the long wharf where the steam boats used to make their landings. This point was shelled early on in the engagements by the gunboats and the wharf destroyed. The coal fell uninjured 10 or 12 feet to the bottom of the river. From this underwater store they fished up all winter, as required (with what they called oyster tongs) as much coal as they needed; although it was hard anthracite coal it seems to have burnt reasonably well in the camp grates.

The first clash of ironclads and the use of torpedoes and sub-marines were spectacular and of great interest to historians and future generals, but they did not really decide the four-year strug-gle. The real battle for existence by the South and for national unity by the North was fought out not in the estuaries or the forts but on the high seas by blockades and blockade runners, and across the country by large land armies, the first great masses of armed amateur soldiers.

4

'A Sawn-Off Roof of a Gabled House Floating on the Water'

BAPTISM OF FIRE—THE FIRST NAVAL ENGAGEMENTS

At sea the most urgent first step for both sides was to gain control of the Chesapeake and the approaches both to Washington and to the Virginian capital of Richmond up the James River. This meant control of the Hampton Roads. Estimates of the initial strength of the Union fleet vary. Admiral Porter, the official historian of the U.S. Navy, reckoned that with a theoretical strength of 35 ships only 8 were available for immediate use in home waters and that these were trying to blockade the whole coast from Newport News to the mouth of the Mississippi, some 3,549 miles. So great were the Union resources, however, that within three months the number had risen to over 100 warships, including 10 or 11 ships of the line, and by the end of 1861 to 264.

On the Confederate side the position was far less healthy. Lacking the industrial capacity for ship-building and with the blockade starting to take effect, their naval strength initially was restricted to those ships, mainly a few schooners and revenue cutters, which by luck were in Confederate ports at the outbreak of war.

According to the Confederate historian, Scharf, this meant a total initial strength of 10 ships and 15 guns. With this meagre number the Confederate navy had to provide jobs for 4 admirals, 10 captains, 31 commanders, and 100 first lieutenants!

The real problem was the desperate shortage of crews, which could only be provided by transfers from the army and it was thus that, as Brain's infrequent letters to my grandfather—his Uncle Fred—at the Bannut Tree House confirm, he found himself on the *Jamestown*. He was certainly there at the time of the famous *Merrimac/Monitor* battle in March 1862, but it is quite obvious that he must have transferred to the *Jamestown* for training as an able seaman before that. So began his career in the Confederate navy, while, at the Norfolk Navy Yard, frantic efforts were being made to salvage sufficient ships and guns to provide at least a defensive if not an attacking force. Even more urgent was the protection of Richmond itself, threatened by the Union ships which were assembling fast at Newport News and already probing the James River. Dredged-up guns had been mounted to form some sort of shore battery, but the ships available for defence of the river were a scanty enough force. They were in fact three in number: the *Yorktown* and the *Jamestown*, both steamers of the New York and Old Dominion line which had by luck been in Richmond when Virginia seceded, and a little tug, the *Teaser*.

The *Yorktown*, a vessel of 1,400 tons, was promptly renamed and referred to in Confederate records as the *Patrick Henry*. She was made the flagship and given rather token armour: one-inch iron plates that were the maximum, it was calculated, that could be put on her without her sinking. In addition she was equipped with 10 of the 15 available guns. The *Jamestown* was a much smaller vessel (she was renamed the *Thomas Jefferson*, but not unnaturally everyone continued to refer to her as the *Jamestown*). Unlike the *Yorktown*, she could not even carry small bits of armour to protect her engine and boilers. The deck was strengthened and it was thought that she might possibly carry two guns. On the little tug, the *Teaser*, they finally managed to mount one gun. The ships' fighting capabilities were almost negligible, but for morale purposes it was at least a little fleet, its potential usefulness being determined more by the dash of the commanders than the fighting power of the ships. Captain Tucker was certainly not the man to make the weakness of his fleet any excuse for not seeking out the enemy.

So on 13 December J. C. Brain found himself steaming down to Newport News to 'feel the enemy', as it was called, and if possible to put a limit to Union gunboat excursions up the James River. Off the point lay the U.S. steamer *Savannah*, the U.S. sloop *Cumberland*, and the U.S. steamer *Louisiana*, and on the land were

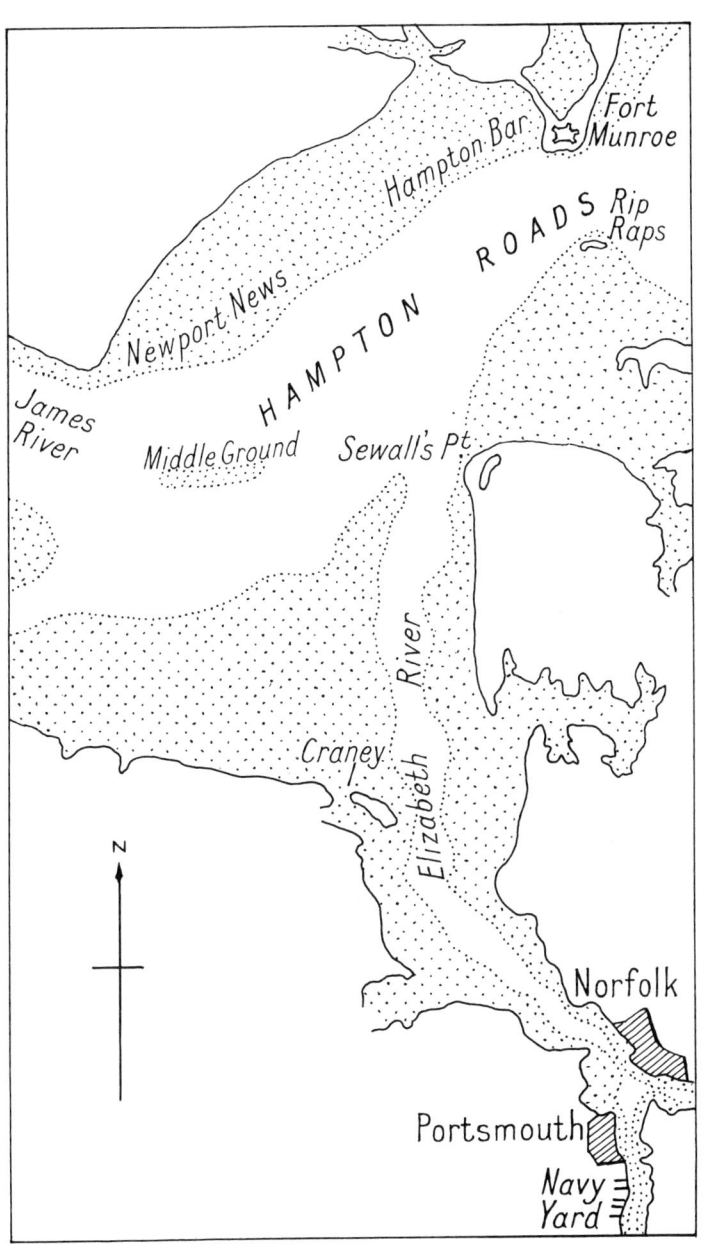

Newport News with the James and Elizabeth Rivers

the heavy batteries of the enemy as well as the battery of light artillery on the banks of the stream.

While the *Jamestown* and the *Teaser* were running about the lower end of the river just out of range of the batteries at Newport News, rumours began to filter up river from the Norfolk Naval Base that the *Merrimac* had actually been raised and was repairable then. She was found to be not too badly damaged, and on Lieutenant John Brook's initiative it was proposed to turn her into one of the first armoured ships afloat. It was thought she would have to be covered with torn-up railway lines made at the Tredegar works at Richmond, as this was the only rolling mill in the South capable of turning out heavy ironware. But it was later found that reasonably suitable plates could be made and this was put through as a rush job, the blacksmiths, strikers, and finishers working without pay until the job was done. In most cases the very tools required by the workmen had to be improvised, and it says a lot for the drive and energy of all concerned that it was finished at all.

The idea was to make very heavy timber walls, sloping at 45°, then cover them with iron plates which would throw off the shot of hostile ships, the armour being continued right down to the waterline. The whole of the charred superstructure was removed, leaving merely a platform for a sort of armoured shed. The original battery of 4 or 5 guns was taken ashore and used by the army and shore batteries, and two seven-inch rifled guns, heavily reinforced round the breech, with three-inch steel bands shrunk on, were installed under the armour plating. These were the first heavy guns to be made in this way and were also the work of Lieutenant Brook. They were the bow and stern guns of the battery. There were also two six-inch guns of the same construction and six nine-inch smooth bore guns on the broadside, making ten in all. Incidentally the vessel is still referred to in the records of both sides as the *Merrimac*, even though the Confederate Navy Board renamed her *Virginia*.

The *Merrimac* had many defects, the worst of them being the engines. These, apart from having been under water for some weeks, were quite unreliable. The whole of her vulnerable stern with the propeller shaft and rudder was entirely unprotected by armour plate of any kind and her draught, over 22 feet, prevented her from going near any vital objective, such as Washington. Her critics multiplied like summer flies and her constructor, John L. Porter, complained of lack of encouragement when he was working on her:

> Hundreds—I may say thousands—asserted she would never float. Some said she would turn bottom side up; others said the crew would suffocate; and the most wise said the concussion and report from her guns would deafen the men. Some said she would not steer; and public opinion generally about here said she would never come out of the dock.

This was too pessimistic, but even her First Lieutenant, Catesby ap R. Jones, who was to command her after Captain Buchanan had been wounded on the first day, said of her, 'She was badly ventilated, very uncomfortable and very unhealthy . . .' Apart from that there were no complaints!

Anyway, these were the sorts of rumours that would be reaching Brain and the James River squadron when, in March 1862, they received orders to move down river and escort this modern miracle to the mouth of the river where she would be let loose upon an astonished enemy!

In theory, of course, the *Merrimac* was on her maiden voyage and should have been doing engine trials and various manoeuvring exercises to accustom her crew to the most extraordinary machine that a poor sailor had ever had to handle. But the necessities of war leave little time for maiden voyages. She left her berth to the cheers of the local inhabitants and with the workmen still aboard finishing off essentials she moved down the river. Next day the workmen were hastily put ashore and the *Merrimac* moved out into open water. By that time Captain Buchanan had discovered, to his horror, that some of her actual defects put even the rumours to shame! Her engines were so ineffective that she could do no more than five knots on a straight course and her steering so defective that it took forty minutes to turn her through 180°. Fortunately nobody else knew this and her first appearance, escorted by the steam tugs *Beaufort* and *Raleigh*, caused a bit of a sensation, not only among Brain and his shipmates in the *James-town* but also to an enemy squadron warned in advance by spies of roughly what to expect. A contemporary report likens her to 'a sawn-off roof of a gabled house floating on the water'.

So unexpected was her arrival that the U.S. Navy frigate *Congress* and the sloop *Cumberland*, at anchor off Newport News, both had the rigging thick with drying clothes, having just had a 'make-do and mend day', when the *Merrimac* hove in sight. The washing disappeared at a rate of knots and the first broadsides were exchanged with the 24-gun sloop *Cumberland*, which was heavily defended by the Union shore batteries of Newport News, by this time within range. The *Merrimac* cut matters short by steaming straight in and ramming the *Cumberland*, Captain Buchanan having had stringent instructions to use the ram as much as possible as there was a frightening shortage of Confederate ammunition. The great weight of metal went through the wooden frigate, to cheers from the *Jamestown* and the *Patrick Henry*, and made a hole big enough to drive a coach and horses through. This, with the simultaneous discharge of her gun, killed 10 men at once and 16 with the next salvo. The blow, which was hardly perceptible on the *Merrimac*, had been received by the *Cumberland* nearly at right angles and she sank shortly afterwards with all flags flying.

The *Merrimac* was by this time under the concentrated fire of about 100 heavy guns at short range, so her armour plating was being well tested. It stood up remarkably well; apart from losing a large chunk of her round prow in the ramming episode, which made her leak slightly, she was untouched. Lieutenant George Morris, of the *Cumberland*, has left us a dramatic account of the way his 'solid shot with the heaviest service charge, struck the terrifying monster and all bounded clear'. The *Merrimac* next turned her attention to the *Congress*, a 50-gun frigate, which very obligingly ran aground and so became a sitting practice target for the *Merrimac*'s guns.

Meanwhile Brain was having his baptism of fire with a vengeance. Captain John R. Tucker led the van in the *Patrick Henry*, closely followed by the *Jamestown* under Lieutenant-Commander Barney and the little *Teaser* under Lieutenant Webb, puffing with all the energy of a short-winded tug. By now the Union shore batteries were firing at leisure, from fixed gun-sights on the three unarmoured little boats, and it is difficult to see how they escaped being blown to pieces. The official history states:

> Their escape was indeed miraculous as they were under a galling fire of solid shot, shell, grape and cannister, a number of which passed clean through the vessels without doing any serious injury except to the *Patrick Henry* through whose boiler a shot passed, scalding to death four persons and wounding others.

The *Jamestown* promptly obeyed a signal to dash in and tow her out of the action. As soon as damages were repaired the *Patrick Henry* returned to her station and continued to perform good service during the remainder of the day.

The vulnerability of these early steamboats is emphasised in a contemporary naval comment:

> A reader should understand that taking a frail steamboat under the fire of heavy guns is a much more dangerous affair than going under fire in an old fashioned ship with sails; for one shot could scarcely disable even a thin walled sailing ship—it would just pass through her—but one shot into a steamer's boiler not only disabled her but slaughtered her crew with the steam.

It must have been an odd sight, especially the minute *Teaser*, solemnly firing her one small gun, and the *Jamestown* carefully firing her two guns at different times in case a simultaneous blast should break up the deck altogether. Odd sight or not, the effectiveness of the squadron is confirmed by a report from Captain Prendergast of the *Congress*, who wrote:

> In the meantime the *Patrick Henry* and the *Jamestown*, rebel steamers, approached us from up the James River, firing with precision and doing us great damage. Our two stern guns were our only means of defence. These were soon disabled, one being dismounted and the other having its muzzle knocked away.

The men were knocked away from them with great rapidity and slaughtered by the terrible fire of the enemy.

As might be expected, the small Confederate boats did not escape unscathed. There is another contemporary report from Captain William Watson of the U.S. gunboat *Dragon* which claimed, 'Arriving at the *Minnesota*, took position and opened fire on the *Patrick Henry* and *Jamestown*, kept it up till dark with good effect. Could plainly see our shells bursting on the enemy.'

The official Confederate history may not be quite impartial, but in this case I don't think Scharf is being inaccurate when he writes:

> The part taken by the little James River squadron is not the least remarkable part of that great fight. It was lost sight of in a battle of iron clad giants but in the days of oak would have been recorded with honourable mention among the acts of bravery and seamanship which illustrate a navy.

There is a lighter side to this action. It is reported from several sources that the Civil War was still not being taken seriously by the bulk of the population. In fact this action was made the excuse for a picnic by a concourse of Confederate matrons on the bluffs overlooking the river. There are accounts of a number of these good ladies meeting together, with their little negro servants carrying large baskets of food, a thing which was to become first very scarce and then almost nonexistent in the later days of the war. It is from one of them, Miss Susan Archer Weiss, that we get another eyewitness account. She was charmed by what she calls the 'saucy *Teaser*' and wrote,

> By this time the *Jamestown* and *Patrick Henry* had joined the *Merrimac*, taking a position which concealed her from our view. We were told afterwards by Federal officers that the little *Teaser*, commanded by Captain Webb, pushed her way in between the *Patrick Henry* and *Jamestown*, advanced close to the shore, fired her one gun in the face of the battery of sixty guns. Probably her insignificance saved her, for now every shot seemed con-

centrated on the *Merrimac*. The air and the very ground on which we stood trembled with the roar of shot and shell. So dense was the smoke that we could discern nothing except the Confederate vessels constantly shifting their position in front of the fleet which was now lying close in shore.

Perhaps I should have mentioned that the waters in these Hampton Roads, where the battles were being fought, are extremely difficult even without having to concentrate on a duel with an enemy ship. A glance at the chart on page 29 will show the large central shoal and many minor hazards, necessitating extremely skilful navigation during the whole of the battle. This, together with bad pilotage, bad luck, or panic, accounts for the fact that three ships of the Union fleet, the *Minnesota*, the *Roanoke* and, the *St. Lawrence* ran aground at least for a time, the *Minnesota* so badly that she could not be refloated for four tides. From their reports, the enemy claimed to have hit the *Jamestown* frequently but certainly not badly enough to disable her, and as night fell she withdrew to her anchorage, looking forward to finishing the job next day. Meanwhile, across the Roads the burning *Congress* lit the sky to remind them that they had something to celebrate.

Had they celebrated a little less wholeheartedly, the crew of the *Jamestown* might have seen another strange shape creeping into the Roads from the Chesapeake by the light of the burning *Congress*, though, I imagine, if they had done so they would have merely put it down to the effect of the rum. But they got a nasty surprise next morning. One of the crew described the new arrival as 'an immense shingle floating on the water with a gigantic cheese box rising from its centre, no sails, no wheels, no smokestack, no guns'. Aboard the *Jamestown* there was considerable argument as to what it really was. Some thought it was a water tank on a raft, others said it was a floating magazine sent to supply the still-grounded *Minnesota*. In fact it was the first Federal ironclad, the *Monitor*, called by some 'Ericsson's folly' after her designer, a Swedish inventor. With insufficient power for the sea passage she had to be towed down from New York by steam tug—somewhat ignominious, but she had proved to be quite uncontrollable in the rough sea for which she was never designed. Despite this, she arrived in the Chesapeake on the evening of the 8th, clearing for action as soon as she got into calmer water, and by 2 a.m. on the 9th was stationed to protect the stranded *Minnesota*.

So the James River squadron, when it came out with the *Merrimac* to finish off the job next day, got a bit of a shock. The *Merrimac* fired at this queer contraption with no visible effect whatever, while according to Mr. Fox, assistant secretary to the Navy who had come down to watch the battle, all the little ships withdrew after the *Monitor* opened fire. They remained in the background fascinated and ready to join in if an opportunity presented itself; indeed the *Jamestown* had to go to the help of the *Merrimac* when she ran aground. But, patently, this was no place for small boats. The *Merrimac* and the *Monitor* fought their now famous duel rather like a couple of old bulls. As many of us will remember from our staff college days, it was to go down in history as the first-ever battle between ironclads and Brain in the *Jamestown* must have had a grandstand view. (See opposite.)

Flag Officer Tatnall who had replaced the wounded Captain Buchanan in the *Merrimac* was a worried man, because his smaller opponent had three great advantages. She only drew 12 feet against the *Merrimac*'s 22 feet and hence had almost twice the amount of water to manoeuvre in. It meant in addition that she could always escape if she got into a tight corner, across bars where the *Merrimac* could not follow. She had much better engines was basically more manoeuvrable, and she had not fought a battle the previous day. The *Merrimac* had incurred enough damage to make her weak engines and steering even more unreliable. Lastly, I think we should not discount the effect on the men of fighting in these very primitive tin boxes. Each shot, as it struck the outer casement armour, would pretty well stun the inhabitants so that at the end of a day they would have been in very poor shape.

In the event, the two ironclads shot away at each other for four hours without doing each other any harm at all as far as could be seen. Starting a mile apart and closing to a hundred yards they quite often grated against each other as one helmsman misjudged the distance, or tried to ram the other. Now and again the *Merrimac* got bored and took pot shots at the *Minnesota* to break the monotony of shooting broadsides at the *Monitor*. The *Merrimac*

The engagement of the *Merrimac* by the *Monitor*—a contemporary artist's impression, reproduced by courtesy of the National Maritime Museum

did at least make contact with her ram but misjudged the angle so badly that she incurred more damage than the *Monitor*. The *Monitor* also attempted a ramming but just missed and her ram slid harmlessly past the *Merrimac*'s vulnerable stern. By midday they had both had enough and the *Monitor* went off into shallow water where the *Merrimac* could not follow.

Next day in the ward rooms and mess decks of the James River squadron there seems to have been considerable discussion as to the best way of dealing with this new phenomenon, the *Monitor*. Ingenious schemes, smacking strongly of the lower deck, were hatched. They included boarding ladders, hoses of scalding steam, hand grenades to be tossed inside the casemate or down the stack, wet sailcloths to stuff down the smokestack, wedges to jam the turret, sheets to throw over the pilot house and blind the helmsman. Later refinements, we find from correspondence, included powder to throw down the smokestack, and turpentine or camphor in glass vessels to smash over the turret with inextinguishable liquid fire to follow. Perhaps it is a pity that neither side had an opportunity to try out any of these ingenious ideas because when the *Merrimac*, after a break for repairs, made her next sortie into the Roads the Union forces decided that the *Monitor* was too precious to be risked in further battle and kept her firmly out of harm's way in the shallows. The little Confederate squadron could, and did, create quite a lot of chaos and the *Jamestown* was particularly active in rounding up stragglers and the smaller shipping and towing them away back up river. The enemy cannot have been too pleased about all this, because the incident was witnessed by English and French men-of-war who happened to be in the bay, in addition to large crowds of spectators who had again flocked on to the beach and cliffs as soon as rumour got around that there was prospect of another battle.

For the next two months Brain and the other raw sailors went on having a lively time nibbling at the much more numerous and powerful Northern naval forces in the Chesapeake and blocking the sea approaches. They themselves had little prospect of any seagoing service, because even the *Merrimac*'s builder was quite certain that she would sink in the first rough sea and the James River squadron had no hope of fighting its way out alone. In any case it had a vital role to play in guarding the main approach to the Confederate capital at Richmond, and the *Merrimac* was entirely dependent on Norfolk Navy Yard as a base.

One thing is clear, this service aboard a steamship, however small or primitive, was to have a profound effect on the young John Clibbon. Up to that time his only experience can have been in sail, and precious little of that. Now he had been pitchforked into steam and the handling of steam ships under all sorts of trying conditions. The experience was to stand him in good stead in the days to come. Steam was exciting; there was still something magical about propelling a large vessel through the water without sails or any outwardly visible means of propulsion—only something going on deep down in the bowels of the ship. He had been allowed to take the wheel of the *Jamestown* for short spells and, I think, it was probably during one of these that he decided on his next move. The naval scene suited him anyway. No more square-bashing, arms drill and forced night marches. He found he preferred a permanent berth, which was always there when he was off watch and wanted to go to bed. But, more fundamentally, the naval life suited his restless temperament and provided much more opportunity for his natural initiative and youthful exuberance.

Ultimately he would not be happy until he had command of his own ship but there seemed little prospect of that just then. Even Brain realised that he had a lot to learn, and that there was considerably more to running a ship than managing the wheel under the mate's eagle eye, or heaving the lead and getting soaked through. Thanks to having been transferred as a gunner, he had escaped any danger of work below decks in the engine room as a technician, stoker or coal-heaver. Meanwhile he was busy with his keen observant mind, taking note of all that went on and especially the weak links in the chain of command.

Then the blow fell—a first blow, maybe foreseen by the 'top brass', but wholly unexpected by victorious officers and ratings who were justly proud of having out-shot and out-manoeuvred the enemy in their two first naval actions. Against superior forces, backed up by land-based forts commanding the narrows, they had destroyed or driven off four 40- or 50-gun ships of the regular

Union navy, sunk the *Cumberland* of 22 guns and disabled four more gunboats. Not a bad two days' work for a converted frigate, two coastal steamers and a minute tug with one gun. The trouble was that the land war was not going so well, and it was soon obvious that Norfolk Navy Base was fast becoming untenable. Without this and its dock, an ironclad like the *Merrimac* was helpless. Unlike the smaller craft she could not make do with a temporary berth up river. Not only was there no dockyard machinery, but she drew 22 feet—an impossible disadvantage in a river full of shoals and narrow passages. She would have merely been a gift to the Northern navy. So, when the naval base at Norfolk had to be abandoned she was destroyed and scuttled— thoroughly, this time.

There was, at first, a complete disbelief among the ships' companies of the little James River squadron—it was so unexpected. Gradually the news was confirmed and sadly accepted as true. The rest of the squadron retired gloomily and thoughtfully up- stream. Now they would fight alone, without their armoured flagship, and the numbers of professional frigates and ships of the line gathered in Hampton Roads at the mouth of the river were increasing every day, not to mention the *Monitor* still lurking somewhere in the shallows off Norfolk News.

The last blow followed swiftly on the astonished heads of the little squadron. The *Jamestown* was to lose her two guns, and with several smaller ships was to be sunk to block access to the river by Drewry's Bluff—the river they had so gallantly defended. This was a shattering end to their hopes, but the guns were needed to man emergency batteries for the defence of the capital. Many were the (quite unjust as it turned out) fulminations against the army boys who had let them down. So absorbed had they been in their own battles, they had hardly noticed that the Union army had been busy around the back areas. They had captured Roanoke Island to the south and, though repulsed at Kernstown by Stone- wall Jackson, had laid siege to Yorktown, just across the narrow peninsula from the James River, on 5 April. There had been rumours of a great battle at Shiloh on 7 April but for many days no one knew which way it had gone. Both sides had been too exhausted to follow up any advantage, their armies being completely green. This had been their first battle and they had shot away at each other for two days and nights, without any tangible result except great piles of dead and wounded. By 4 May, Yorktown had to be evacuated and the next day saw the enemy at the gates of the old Virginian capital of Williamsburg, now a pleasant village.

There is one last and rather touching result of the final bottling up and scuttling of the *Merrimac*. Just before this happened Colonel Blanton Duncan had appealed for funds with which to build another ironclad ship under supervision of the Navy Department. The result was this charming letter in the *Richmond Dispatch* on 28 March:

To the Editor: Please state in your paper that the ladies of Williamsburg, impressed with the importance of every effort to defend our country, have organised a society for the purpose of building an ironclad gun boat to aid in protecting our coast from depredation and our Capital from attack by water. Their efforts so far have been crowned with signal success. It is to be hoped that with like enthusiasm their countrywomen throughout the State will at once form similar societies for the purpose of obtaining funds for this object which if promptly undertaken and actively carried out may prove of incalculable benefit to our state and country.

By the energy, industry and patriotism of the women of Virginia and the influence they can wield over those who are able to contribute to so laudable a design, a fund may soon be collected sufficient to place upon our waters a valuable ally of the mail-clad *Virginia* [*Merrimac*] the best defence of our harbours and rivers from the attacks of an insolent enemy whose naval power has already inflicted heavy blows upon our coast.

The ladies of Williamsburg therefore earnestly invite the co-operation of their sisters throughout the state and recommend the immediate adoption of such means to secure the desired result. Contributions from societies or individuals may be forwarded to either of the following ladies:

Mrs. Judge B. Tucker
Mrs. W. W. West
Mrs. Ro. Saunders
and six others.

The Ladies Defence Association was then formed at Richmond and Mrs. Maria G. Clofton was made president. Well, it can never be said the South went under for lack of the will to survive!

I cannot leave the Norfolk Navy Yard without one last backward look. As the tired little garrison burned it, thoroughly this time, on 9 May, they managed to save two little gunboats, the *Nansimond* and the *Hampton*, which were got out by installing 'saw mill' engines at the last minute. Captain W. H. Parker wrote: 'When they got under way there was such a wheezing and blowing that one would suppose all hands had been attacked with the asthma or heaves.' No engines could be devised for the remaining two and they had to be scuttled.

It was a sad end to high hopes, but, as so often in history, command of the seas had been decisive. The Union navy had been able to carry and to land troops anywhere at no notice for surprise attacks, while the raw Confederate armies had to walk all round the estuaries to meet emergencies.

A Knight of the Golden Circle

SECRET SERVICE—AND SO TO PRISON

So here was Gunner Brain, about 12 May 1862, back to square one, without a ship and posted again to shore duties at Drewry's Bluff to serve the naval guns hastily mounted from the erstwhile James River squadron. He found himself under Captain F. Chatard, C.S.N., who, one gathers from family gossip, he did not like much. I suspect the Captain was a disciplinarian of the old school.

The garrison beat off a determined first attack on 15 May and thereafter battery duty became rather boring, especially as Brain had only to look over the parapet to see his first love, the *Jamestown*, lying in a few fathoms with her funnel and one mast still above water. He may even have remembered his commanding officer Lieutenant Barney's farewell speech when he assembled the little steamer's crew on deck for the last time. 'Every officer and man on board the ship performed his whole duty evincing a courage and fearlessness worthy of the cause for which we are fighting.'

He may have regarded this a little more cynically than some of his mates, but it made him feel good. Though he had no background of naval tradition behind him in his ancestry, coming, as we have seen, from a solid middle-class family to whom a day's offshore fishing was still an adventure, the months on the *Jamestown* and his baptism of fire had obviously done something for him.

For the first time in his life he was recognised as an individual and allowed to work things out on his own initiative. Only aboard a small ship is there scope for, indeed a necessity for, a certain amount of delegated authority; the rudimentary system of communications enforced that, if nothing else. In his short taste of the army, supervision had been both inept and continuous. But in the navy, though professional officers might have looked upon their crop of amateur sailors from a great height, they were still of the clan—part of a tight ship's company that had to work together or sink. They were professionals and they were good ones.

The army was very different. The few professionals were lost in the masses of enthusiastic 'makee-learns' from the cotton plantations and hill farms. Neither officers nor men, including the much-maligned 'gentleman privates', had ever heard a shot fired in anger. Hence the patriotic enthusiast tended to enlist as a private —a sort of inverted snobbery—while the rich, hard-riding fool was influential enough to organise a commission. This meant he could bring his own servant with him to ensure his comfort and groom his horse. Later the horses had to be eaten and the more sensible grooms ran the black market in foodstuffs.

I do not think cousin Brain liked horses. He certainly had little use for their owners, especially at close quarters in that most soul destroying existence, manning a battery which, in between short periods of intense and noisy activity, had nothing to fire at for weeks on end, nothing to do but endless gun drill and polishing and lugging ammunition up rough roads. The only consolation was that he made new friends among the naval personnel, especially a character called Parr, a doctor in civilian life, who crops up from time to time in this narrative as Brain's number one. Anyway Brain must have decided that there was really no future in battery life and as there was no apparent prospect of the Confederates providing another ship for him to serve in, he had to see what he could do on his own initiative. This, as we shall see, was not negligible, though regrettably unorthodox.

We very soon get news of him. According to the *Pictorial History of the Civil War,* he succeeded fairly rapidly in talking his way out of the dull routine of naval battery duty and reappears as one of the 'Knights of the Golden Circle'. This, according to a column in the *New York Times,* was 'the secret service organisation of the Rebel Government operating in the Northern State'.

Brain's own motives for seeking a change have already been discussed and were elementary enough, though perhaps ingenious in execution. It was quite a shrewd move on the part of the Confederate Government. Brain knew his way about the enemy territory by now, as we have seen, and I imagine there were not many volunteers from the regular officer corps for secret service work! Brain must have shot fairly rapidly through the non-commissioned ranks and was now listed in the only official, surviving Register of the Provisional Navy of the Confederate States as a 'Master not in line of Promotion'. The exact date of his commissioning as acting second lieutenant cannot be determined, owing to the almost total destruction of Confederate naval records after final defeat. All I can say is that from about this time references in newspapers begin to speak of him as Lieutenant Brain. It seems, in any case, a natural thing for a government to do before launching a member of its naval personnel upon a secret service mission in enemy territory. To the Northern papers he remains, of course, a 'reckless' or 'accomplished' scoundrel, according to taste, and later simply 'a Pirate', like the rest of the Confederate privateers.

His 'undercover' activity turns out to be the production of Railway Guides, of all things. He was probably making use of the only skill (drawing and engraving) bequeathed to him by his feckless father. For a time, not only did the work of the Knights of the Golden Circle flourish but, we gather, so did the much more personally profitable propaganda on behalf of the Union State railways, which were rapidly being pushed westwards and southwards in aid of the war effort. But, sadly, I have to relate that like all good things these activities come to an end—in this case an abrupt one.

In a long article, the *New York Times* states 'He [Brain] was arrested in the South West where he was engaged on Illustrated Railway Guides and charged with assisting the Confederates and Committed to Fort Lafayette'. Lafayette, in Massachusetts, was what we would now call a 'top security' prison for special P.O.W.s and important agents or spies or Knights of the Golden Circle— whatever you like to call them—and there he remained firmly incarcerated for 'some months', at least much relieved, one imagines, at not having been shot.

However, it was not in Brain's nature to sit down and mope.

So it is not surprising to hear from the *Quebec Mercury* that 'He secured his release through Lord Lyons, on his engaging to leave the United States'. The excuse was, apparently, that he was technically not a Confederate citizen but a British subject with a Confederate commission only. It sounds a bit slim and I can only guess that the *Quebec Mercury* reporter had not been able to dredge up the whole story. The 'engagement' to leave the United States does not trouble him much because the country has got too hot to hold him, not for the first time in his short life, and his usefulness as a Confederate secret service agent is obviously finished for the present.

We next hear that he has turned up in Montreal, just across the border; not very far, you may feel, but he has complied with the undertaking, technically. He is, again, a little short of money and as it is a long way to Richmond, with its unattractive prospect of more naval battery duty, he decides like a sensible fellow to make some money first—in his own inimitable, if questionable, way! Let the *Quebec Mercury*'s reporter tell the story in his own words.

He [Brain] came to Montreal where by some agents he got introduced to the authorities of the Grand Trunk and undertook the publication of a Grand Trunk Railway Guide, announcing Mr. John Lovell, of Montreal as his printer. Mr. Lovell, finding that Brain was collecting large sums for subscriptions and advertisements, refused to allow him to use his name unless he gave a satisfactory deposit, which Brain refused. While here, he employed engravers to do the work for his book which he did not pay for.

Before he left, he patronised us and some of our contemporaries to the extent of some hundred dollars. Hence he proceeded to Quebec and some of the lower ports where he repeated his operations. We next heard from him in Liverpool and Manchester, England where he was levying contributions with a good deal of success. Steps were taken by Mr. Lovell and others to warn parties against him and it appears that Mr. Brain again flitted westwards.

Having acquired some money, though in a most reprehensible

way, and spent a few memorable nights with his uncle and faintly disapproving aunts at the Bannut Tree House, he returned quite cheerfully to the war—with his thoughts still more firmly set on a command of his own, however difficult that was going to be to achieve with the remainder of the Confederate fleet bottled up in the James River. In his youthful view, the proper place for a sailor, even an amateur one, was in a ship at sea.

Back in Richmond, his worst fears are confirmed. Half-jokingly, he is told he had better go and find a ship for himself and that fairly quickly, or there would be a firm posting back to his old battery on Drewry's Bluff.

6

'Prowling Around for Coal'

BRAIN CAPTURES THE *CHESAPEAKE*

Apart from some action around the Mississippi and the defensive squadron on the James River, Confederate naval activity was by this time, November 1863, limited to blockade running and privateering. The first was concerned with bringing war materials into and taking cotton out from the two Southern ports still open, Wilmington and Charleston. It was profitable work and, as we shall see later, by no means unexciting, but of course you had first to own, or be appointed to the command of, a ship. In any case, I think Brain was always drawn to the more spectacular job of privateering—setting out on the high seas in his own ship with no instructions except to do the maximum damage he could to enemy shipping, by capture, seizing of valuable cargoes, and, when necessary, by destruction. Again, if you had a ship you would have little difficulty in being accepted for the 'volunteer navy' provided you could produce satisfactory evidence as to 'character, competence and means'.

After two world wars even the civilian population has now become aware of the importance of the destruction of merchant shipping as a weapon of war, in order to starve the enemy into surrender. In 1860 people had already forgotten that this was practised during the Napoleonic War and were probably quite unaware that the Western powers had decided, during the Crimean War, that it was improper and had signed conventions renouncing it. I do not know why the United States had not signed the convention but this may account for the fury of the Government and almost hysterical outbursts of the Northern newspapers when the weapon was used against the North by the South.

So important was privateering, however, that the Confederate Government was busy persuading British and French shipyards to build ships for this purpose, apart from adapting any captured prizes that were suitable.[6] By this time, the operations of the privateers were the only tangible successes which could be set against the invariably gloomy reports of army defeats, and upon their ultimate harvest the outcome of the war might well depend. The *Alabama* and the *Florida* and others had already had considerable success and their captains, like Semmes and Maffitt,[7] were by then national heroes. But, as Brain knew only too well, if new ships became available there was a long list of regular naval officers with unassailable Annapolis backgrounds waiting their turn for every prize, however small, that could be manoeuvred across the Gulf Stream and through the thick curtain of patrolling cruisers blockading each port. If a mere master, acting lieutenant were ask for to a command, there would be an astonished silence.

So, he would have to help himself and this meant acquiring an enemy ship, already armed if possible. If not it could be taken to a neutral port where certain discreet gentlemen were quite ready to sell suitable guns without asking too many awkward questions— if the price was right. Raids on the enemy main shipping lanes could then begin. Somehow he managed to make contact again with an old buddy of his from the *Jamestown*, Lieutenant H. A. Parr, the ex-doctor, and by mid-autumn of that year (1863) Brain had managed to collect quite a little party of old friends from the James River squadron days. Among them were Second Lieutenant D. Collins, sailing master George Rowson and two gentlemen by the names of McKinnon and Seely whom we know less about.

Then Brain goes to see the Navy Board with an audacious plan for seizing an ocean-going Union steamer, not in some remote port in the Gulf of Mexico or the West Indies but at the very centre and hub of Northern naval commercial activity—New York. He argues that no one will be expecting a Confederate naval party in this enemy stronghold. However sceptical the Navy Board may have been, they could not afford to throw away even a remote, and what may have seemed to them crazy, chance of adding to their very small navy.

So, as we later learn from the *New York Tribune*, the newly-promoted lieutenant is provided with a copy of his commission and instructions from the Naval Department at Richmond. The *Tribune* quotes him as saying, 'I received orders from the Department at Richmond to go North with my command, consisting of seventeen officers and men and take passage in a steamer with the purpose of capturing it upon the high seas.' He later adds, 'After seizing the vessel I was to proceed to Seal Cove in the Island of Grand Manan, off the coast of Maine, for coal and there to hand the vessel over to Capt. John Parker, my superior officer.'

He was also given Letters of Marque. These were vital, especially when the Northern press and Government were calling all Southern privateers, however officially commissioned and authorised, pirates and murderers. Anybody without these precious documents would have got short shrift even in neutral courts like the British in Canada. By March 1863 both sides were issuing Letters of Marque—each one duly approved by the President and ratified by Congress. The practice had been common since the sixteenth century and thereafter covered many illustrious names from Drake to the United States' own Paul Jones. The Letters of Marque issued by Jefferson Davis, the President of the Confederate States, ran:

To all who shall see these presents, greeting:
Know ye, that by virtue of the power vested in me by law I have commanded and do hereby authorize the vessel called the ... [then follows description of vessel, captain, and crew] ... to act as a private armed vessel in the service of the Confederate States, on the high seas, against the United States of America, their ships, vessels, goods and effects and those of her citizens, during the tendency of the war now existing etc. . . .

Given under my hand and seal of the
Confederate States. Dated and signed
Jefferson Davis and countersigned by
the Secretary of State

There must have been one little snag. As Brain had not been able to select his ship in advance, let alone guarantee successful capture of it, the name of the vessel would have been omitted on his documents. I can only imagine it was felt that he would be able to copy the writing of the clerk who had written in his name and those of his crew at the time the President signed it. This was the one flaw in his armour.

The instructions to hand over to Captain Parker if successful remain something of a mystery to me even after many months' research among official documents. I can understand the Navy Board feeling that Lieutenant Brain, at twenty-three, was still a bit young to be in sole charge of a sort of commando expedition which aimed first at capturing a fastish enemy steamship, then arming it abroad or by running the blockade into a Confederate port, and lastly operating on the high seas as a commissioned privateer. But what puzzles me is why the raw lieutenant was thought to be capable of carrying out the first and by far the most difficult part of the operation—seizing a suitable ship (however much it may have been his idea)—and yet not capable of carrying out the much less dangerous parts of the operation. Secondly, I cannot think why the senior officer went off to a nice safe berth in neutral Canada, near Grand Manan Island in New Brunswick, under the excuse that he was arranging for coaling, while Brain set off with his party into enemy territory to effect the capture on his own.

Lastly, the choice of Parker (who does not appear in the only Confederate Navy list to survive) is incomprehensible. I can only think no regular officer could be persuaded to volunteer for such a hare-brained scheme, because research reveals that Parker was a pretty suspect character. True, he had been captain of the Confederate steam privateer *Retribution*. This sounds very grand until one finds out that she started life as the tugboat *Uncle Ben* on Lake Erie. The U.S. Navy took her to sea, but she was so slow that she got lost on the way past the Carolinas. The North Carolinians took one look at her, put her engines into a new ironclad they were building, and sold the hull as a wreck. Parker patched her up, blocked up the old propeller shaft hole, stuck in two masts and renamed her the *Retribution*. She was credited in the official list with three prizes: the brig *I. P. Ellicote* (10 January 1863), the schooner *Hanover*, value $11,630.00 on 31 January, and the brig *Emily Fisher*, value $9,352.26, on 10 February. But the gallant captain had abandoned the good ship *Retribution* in Nassau some months previously, quite irrevocably unseaworthy. In any case his name was not Parker at all; it was V. G. Locke.

It says a lot for Brain that we never hear a word of complaint or even a disloyal comment when things went wrong. However, some time in late November Brain and his men slipped through the Confederate lines and across the Rappahannock, while Captain Parker went north to wait safely in Canada for the outcome of Brain's attempt.

We soon hear of Brain's party again from official sources in New York—in the heart of enemy country—disguised as longshoremen. They were, understandably enough, busy drinking their way painlessly from tavern to tavern along the waterfront where the bustle of shipping was loudest and the tongues wagged most freely. If you had chanced along, you might have fallen into conversation with a charming young English officer who would have revealed, after a couple of schnapps, that he was Captain Chilborough and furthermore that he was the agent of a certain well-known English steamboat company, accredited to the United States Government who, he would explain, were understandably anxious to negotiate the purchase of shipping to replace depredations by those unmentionable Confederate raiders—'pirates' the law-abiding New York citizens called them.

P.O.W. authorities at Fort Lafayette, away up in Massachusetts, would have recognised him as Brain, J. C., Master, acting Lieutenant, C.S.N.—but that was a chance he had to take.

So the prospect of a ship was beginning to materialise, even in the most unlikely place in the New World. It was a daring scheme and highly dangerous, seeing that all masters and crews of ships sailing under the Union flag in coastal waters were fully armed and protected by a screen of warships and gunboats of the local patrolling squadron. Brain's idea was quite simple and wholly consistent with his matter-of-fact thinking and ability to go straight to the core of the problem without bothering with non-essentials. Each of his crew had been promised $500 in addition to his naval pay as soon as any suitable vessel which might be captured was safely berthed in either of the two Confederate ports.

Brain had been considering the possibility of commandeering a large fishing smack and boarding a suitable ship after dark, perhaps from the offshore banks where ingoing and outgoing ships hove-to for the purpose of picking up or dropping the harbour pilots. It was attractive but there were too many things that could go wrong at the last minute. So, much simpler, they would choose a fast passenger ship, go aboard in the normal way, brazen it out and seize the ship from within. The last operation would need very accurate timing and careful planning, but it seemed to promise better.

This period of watching and weighing up all possibilities is a tense and trying time for the crew members mixing day by day in the waterside taverns with the officers and crews of the blockading cruisers coming thankfully off patrol duty after a week or so of tossing to and fro in a searing north-east wind. It is already late in the fall, and ashore the icy wind straight from the Canadian Arctic wastes shrivels up everything in its path along the cobbled quays.

After a careful survey, Brain chooses a fairly new, fastish steamship, the S.S. *Chesapeake*. Though somewhat larger and more seaworthy, her engines are not unlike those of the old *Jamestown* with which he is familiar. She is passenger-carrying as well as a cargo ship (which conveniently settles her mode of capture) and is commanded by Captain Willetts. Brain knows the officers will be armed, and in addition there will be an armed guard.

I imagine Captain Willetts is both surprised and pleased to have most of his passenger accommodation taken up at the last minute, because he is on a routine run to Portland (Maine) and the weather on the foggy New England coasts in December isn't exactly conducive to full passenger lists. And taken up it is; Brain has decided not to gamble on being able to 'persuade' the Union crew to continue to man the ship on its way south to a Confederate port, if all goes well, so he has enlarged his own numbers from the original five to seventeen.

This was 5 December 1863, and, I suppose, such were the wartime conditions with troops on leave and folk hurrying hither and thither that the duty officer of the watch in the *Chesapeake* did not think there was anything odd about some of the passengers

5

coming aboard with paper parcels under their arms instead of the usual luggage. He might have felt differently had he known that each paper parcel contained a pistol, ammunition, and a pair of handcuffs.

But let me quote again from the *New York Times* which, a few days later, had a lengthy column under banner headlines. Apparently the arrival of the Confederate party had not passed entirely unnoticed—or perhaps it was just hindsight!

The *Chesapeake*, which belongs to the Cromwell line, left pier No. 9 on the afternoon of Saturday December the 6th. Her cargo was not large and she was carrying 24 passengers and was bound for Portland Maine.

For some time past a number of strangers had been noticed at a hotel in Jersey City, 'arrivals from Nassau'. They kept themselves together and appeared to be curious and observant of all things. There was nothing, however, that could create enough suspicion in regard to them to justify investigation. It was known that their baggage was unusually heavy but that, at the time, attracted but passing attention.

On Saturday morning, some hours before the sailing of the *Chesapeake*, eight of these men purchased at the office of the line in West Street, tickets for Portland Me. Their appearance was that of persons in very modest circumstances and they aided that impression by carrying their own trunks, each one of which, it was observed was almost too much for two men to get along with. When the trunks were on board they were watched with vigilance by a portion of the men. The result shows that they were fitted with both guns and ammunition.

After the first batch had secured their tickets and taken on board their luggage, eight more made their appearance and secured tickets; meanwhile the *Chesapeake* had left her dock, and these had to row into the stream to take her. When they reached the vessel they neither recognised nor were recognised by their comrades.

This is all rather pedestrian journalism, as it is always very easy to remember suspicious characters and movements some days

The S.S. *Chesapeake* (Brain's first capture)—from a contemporary drawing

after being alerted by a startling event, or with hindsight after interviewing members of the crew. There cannot have been much to arouse suspicion at the time or the Confederates would have been challenged, because the port was stiff with police and naval guards, in addition to which all the *Chesapeake*'s officers and watch-keepers were full armed.

Anyway, the *Chesapeake* duly sailed on the tide in the afternoon with Captain Willetts who, no doubt, found his distinguished young passenger, Captain Chilborough, very good company. They talked about the steamship line for which he was an agent and Chilborough explained he preferred 'this way of reaching Portland as the quickest and cheapest'. Brain had done his home-work thoroughly and knew the main facts about the ship, but each vessel, especially in those days, has a separate personality and needs to be humoured. Also he had to know just where every-thing, including the armoury and ammunition store, was located. His officers and crew among the passengers were also busy learn-ing their way around without exciting suspicion.

Next day Willetts was only too pleased to take Captain Chil-borough with him on 'Captain's Rounds'. His guest was especially interested in the engine room, not surprisingly, and was perhaps a thought too persistent about the actual fuel consumption at various speeds. But it was put down to his profession and Willetts, like any other skipper, was too proud of his ship and too compli-mented to notice anything strange.

The *Chesapeake*, built in 1853, was of 160 tons, drawing about 11 feet. She was solidly built of oak and, as Brain could see, was schooner-rigged—a rig he was by then well acquainted with from the handling point of view. He was lucky that the engine was not unlike that in the old *Jamestown* in design, an inverted, direct-acting type, developing 240 h.p. There was one 40-inch cylinder with a 42-inch piston, according to the *New York Times* account. This gave a cruising speed, under power alone, of 11 knots, with a speed of 14 knots for short periods. What concerned Brain much more was that he found there were only 30 tons of coal in the bunkers—sufficient for only about three days' steaming! The sail area was a little small for her size, and, as Captain Willetts explained, 'not to be depended on without auxiliary power'.

The coast of Long Island, all ninety miles of it, slips by and a course is set which will leave Nantucket Island just to port, avoiding the complications of the banks between it and Martha's Vineyard. The second night, that of 7 December, they had just rounded Cape Cod and, being about twenty miles north-north-east of it, set course direct for Portland, when Brain struck at 1.30 a.m. He chose the time well, before dawn, when morale would be at its lowest and organised chaos at its most effective.

There is a long and, as one might expect, very biassed and extravagantly worded account of the seizure given by Captain Willetts and his officers to the *New York Times*[8] after they had been put ashore safely so I will quote the more coherent passages and extract the facts from the remainder.

> It was on Sunday evening that the deed was accomplished. For some hours before, the sixteen seem to have subsided in their curiosity and to have no other feeling (like the rest of the passengers) than anxiety to reach their destination. The officers and crew, save those on duty, had retired and all was quiet and the night dark and the time propitious. They had so dispersed their members that there was little hope of overpowering them. [By 1.30 a.m.] they were posted, armed with six-barrelled revolvers at the door of each stateroom and (at a signal) the watch on the upper deck were secured so they could give no alarm.

Then follows a long and contradictory account of how members of the crew tried to thwart the attempt of the 'Pirates' (as all Confederate personnel were called in Union newspapers) to complete the 'takeover'. The Union captain and crew had been caught absolutely bending and were trying desperately in their statements to the *New York Times* reporters to save face and pave the way for the official enquiry which was hanging over their heads. Some facts do correspond with evidence from other sources.

Brain had his crew so well drilled that in no time at all after the *Chesapeake* had been declared a Confederate prize, the crew were disarmed and manacled. The officers were given the choice of remaining free on parole or being put in irons and most, including Captain Willetts, chose the former.

This was, after all, the first military operation of the war which Lieutenant Brain had initiated, planned, and supervised entirely on his own and not as a member of a ship's crew. Not only had it been a complete success but it had been so efficient that it was carried out almost bloodlessly. There was only one killed, the second engineer, and there were a few minor casualties, including the first mate who put up a spirited resistance and was shot in the jaw, and the second mate who received leg injuries. The rest of the crew were put in irons (the handcuffs had proved their worth!) except the Chief Engineer, Joseph Johnson, his assistant, Augustus Starbeck, and three firemen, who were forced at gunpoint to run the vessel until Brain's engineers felt competent to take over. One of the firemen, Richard Tracy, was a bit obstinate, I gather but soon decided discretion was the better part of valour.

And now, a point that was later to become very important emerges. As soon as Brain had control of the ship he sent for Captain Willetts, who had been confined to his cabin under guard, and showed him his Letters of Marque and orders for the seizure of the ship. Not only did Willetts not spot that the name of the ship was a later insertion but he accepted as genuine the signatures of Jefferson Davis (President) and Secretary Mallory. These signatures were well known by then and Willetts would have been quick to spot any flaw in these unusual Letters of Marque. So, subsequent newspaper screams of piracy and murder were complete wartime propaganda. It was during this meeting that the second engineer was shot. Captain Willetts recorded, 'Of a sudden, the vessel stopped its movement and immediate enquiry was made as to the reason.' Apparently the second engineer, having first agreed to co-operate and been given his freedom on parole, attempted to sabotage the machinery and put the engine room out of action. As he had somehow re-armed himself, there was a fight and he came off second best, but the engine room was fortunately preserved.

The ship then being the Confederate prize steamship *Chesapeake*, no doubt her new acting captain was dying to run up the Confederate flag in his first command; but that, he realised, would have been asking for trouble at that juncture. So long as she maintained course for Portland and looked normal to any passing naval cruiser, she was probably safe from interference unless she was unlucky enough to undergo a routine search.

Having succeeded in his first self-planned venture, Brain was probably cursing his instructions to steam away to the north to pick up friend Parker. The blockading cruisers were thinning out and by standing out to sea before turning south he would be unlucky if he could not capture a coal brig to supplement his meagre three days' supply, now partly used anyway, and make the latitude of Wilmington. From there the drill would be to creep along the shore, which was much of it steep-to, where the blockading cruisers would not dare to follow. That would be in the competent hands of sailing master George Rowson, who was as familiar with the coastal wrecks, lit signals and shoals as with the proverbial back of his hand.

However, not the enemy cruisers but the problem of coaling was always the main worry in those early days of fantastically greedy furnaces. Brain must have been doing some pretty intensive calculations, with the help of the 'impressed' chief engineer and his own engineer. It would be about 1,000 sea miles from the Canadian border to Wilmington, the nearer Confederate port— that is, if he kept his promise to pick up Parker and hand over command of his first prize ship captured entirely on his own initiative. In addition Parker would collect most of the prize money, when they got back to the Confederacy, and this would be considerable on any basis. The *Chesapeake* would then be armed and equipped as a regular government privateer and the big question mark was, would Brain be appointed to command her or would it be a regular officer, or Captain Parker?

There were clearly two alternatives. Brain must have been sorely tempted to forget about Parker, get a good offing, and capture a coal brig before running for Wilmington direct, or at least Bermuda (600 miles) where more coal would be available, at a price. He might have to sell cargo to pay for it but, although this was illegal, it would most certainly be overlooked if he brought a nice new ship in to add to the Confederate States' dwindling fleet. In any case, he would have to take the risk of being allowed to continue in command but there were growing precedents for this —if not a tacit understanding that 'findings was keepings'—*pour encourager les autres.*

The other course was, his duty bound, to obey his Navy Board instructions and find Captain Parker, hoping to recoal in Canada on the quiet. Not all coal was of suitable quality like the Welsh anthracite, which was the best. For instance, the North Carolina soft coal they had had to use at the end of Brain's time in the *Jamestown* had been appalling and smoked terribly. Coal like that not only sooted-up everything but alerted enemy cruisers for miles around to any blockade runner's presence.

I think it says a lot for the integrity of this young lieutenant, to whom history has never really done justice, that he put aside the glamour of taking his own ship back to Wilmington and obediently turned north for the rendezvous. The irony of fate was that this decision was to prove fatal to the enterprise.

Meanwhile, there was plenty to occupy him and his officers. It must be remembered that this was his first command and he was still only twenty-three—a pleasant age to be alive, especially in an exciting world at war, where unlimited possibilities appeared to exist for tweaking the tail of the third most powerful and efficient navy in the world. Whatever we may think of Brain's private life, he was a born leader. It is easy to command respect and maintain discipline on the barrack square behind rows of sergeant majors, or even in a well-ordered battle, but commando-type operations need a bit extra in personal magnetism. Even the enemy paper, the *New York Tribune*, described Brain as a 'tall, straight and commanding looking personage'.

Anyway it must have taken the best part of a day to get used to the ship, determine which of the Union prisoners were to be left locked up and which enlisted in the Confederate navy, however temporarily, to work as engineers, stokers or coal passers. We know from later evidence that Brain was meticulous in laying down standard Confederate rates of pay and seeing that these were promptly honoured—in good United States currency from the ex-purser's office!

Shipping would be fairly thick, as the whole of the British/ Canadian commercial traffic used this lane and it was patrolled,

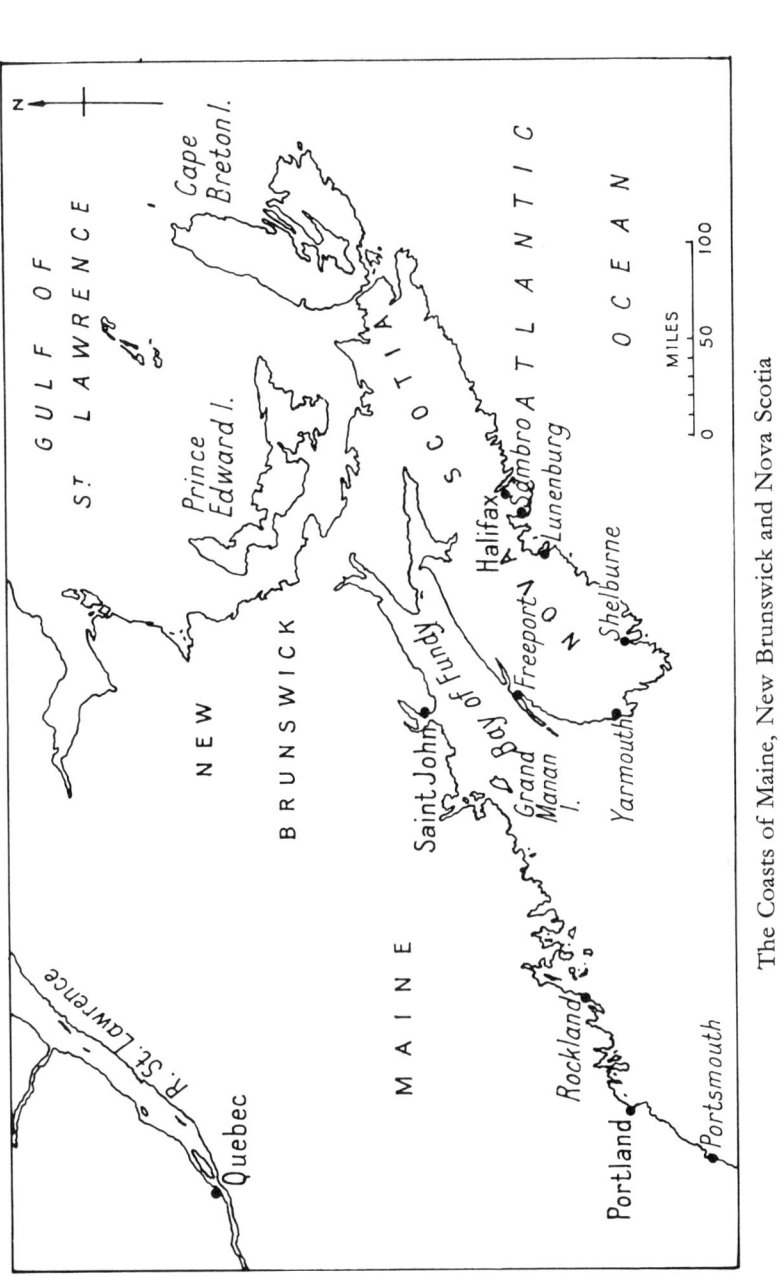

The Coasts of Maine, New Brunswick and Nova Scotia

though not nearly as heavily as in the New York area. Hence it was vital to keep the outside of the vessel as normal as possible and prevent the former crew from making any signals or doing anything that would have attracted the attention of passing ships. By dawn next day they would have passed Portland and made a 45° change of course to the east-nor'-east for Grand Manan Island. From then on, the *Chesapeake*'s non-arrival at Portland would have been reported, and very soon mechanical trouble in a busy sea lane in quite reasonable weather would have been ruled out as a reason.

About mid-afternoon a call is made at the Island, just over the Canadian border, but there is no sign of Captain Parker or his party. I can only guess at the explanation Lieutenant Brain gave for the *Chesapeake*'s unscheduled arrival at the Island. There must have been a hurried consultation on board. Two things stuck out like sore thumbs. First, some coal brigs must be captured, and that fairly rapidly. The three days' supply was almost exhausted even after economical running and assistance from the sails. For the run to Wilmington some of the cargo would have to be jettisoned to make room for extra coal, or—a thought which must have occurred to Brain—sold to pay for the extra load of good British anthracite which could be bought, with any luck, in a Canadian port.

The second uncomfortable thought was that by now the alarm would have gone out, certainly to the Federal Navy cruisers and perhaps more slowly to nearby Canadian ports. This put a premium on a quick coaling before the news spread or the capture of a full coal brig. The nearest port on the mainland where coal would be certain to be had was St. John, just over a hundred miles up the Bay of Fundy in New Brunswick. Furthermore, there was a vastly greater chance of overtaking and capturing a coal ship by keeping close in shore.

As a matter of fact, had Brain known it, wires were already buzzing furiously and during the next few days an absolute deluge of panicky rumours and reports built up in the United States' and Canadian papers—not least in the *New York Times*, which had by 14 December banner headlines reading,

THE PIRATE CHESAPEAKE AT SEA
SHE IS PROWLING AROUND FOR COAL.

The leading column begins,

> A despatch from Halifax this morning states, she is supposed
> to be on the track of some coal vessels. . . . Few more suggestive
> acts in regard to the desperation of the Rebels, have been com-
> mitted than the seizure of the *Chesapeake* from this port. It
> startled and alarmed the entire country and awakened the
> authorities to the dangers that have for a long while existed
> and are now developed. The number of 'arrivals from Nassau',
> the number of blockade runners shipping crews which have
> been discharged in our Northern Ports, all doubly dyed with
> treason and detestation of the Union . . . have been enough to
> man a fleet.

A glorious bit of typical newspaper sensationalism and scare-
mongering, you may think. But it has its point. It shows the effect
on national morale of small events like the unexpected capture of
one steamer right under the noses of the naval authorities in a
'safe area'. The report goes on to say, 'The effect on our shippers
has been discouraging and a feeling of insecurity prevails with
abundant reason. Without the utmost detective precaution, the
Chesapeake affair is but the beginning of the end.' Newspaper
exaggeration this may be, but it is what the population is going to
read and it shows very clearly the psychological effect of the capture as being far greater than the actual benefit of a possible
addition to the tiny Confederate fleet. And by this time the Confederacy needed all the morale boosting it could get.

The immediate effect as far as Brain was concerned was that six
Federal cruisers were diverted from their routine duties to concentrate on locating and recapturing the *Chesapeake* before she
escaped to Bermuda and thence to a Southern port. They knew
also, of course, that she would be short of coal in a few days at
full head of steam and one way or another would have to coal
soon. Damping down the furnaces would spin it out a bit, but not

for long. All coal ships where possible were recalled or left in port. Brain had heard that Captain John Wilkinson, one of the most famous and experienced privateers and blockade runners, had achieved 'An excellent head of steam by using cotton saturated with spirits of turpentine'; but unfortunately Brain's cargo did not include any cotton bales, not having come from the South.

Wilkinson also recalled one occasion when

> We had fired so hard that the very planks on the bridge were almost scorching hot and my feet were nearly blistered. I put them out of the window to cool after taking off slippers and socks . . . later, one of the passengers, Miss Lucy G. came on the bridge and said, 'Ah Captain, I see we are all safe now.'

But to return to the *Chesapeake*. The coal crisis was looming unpleasantly. Just off St. John a pilot boat was spotted coming out and Brain decides to brazen it out and see what arrangements could be made. He could at least test the local reaction and after that he would have to play it by ear. The pilot could be added to the collection of prisoners if he was awkward, though in the event this was not necessary.

This decision was just as well, for, as the pilot boat prepared to round up to the steamer, there in the stern sheets was Captain Parker—late of the *Retribution*—ready to take command now all the rough stuff was over. The pilot, apparently had a bit of a shock when he learned what sort of passenger he had ferried out to what he probably, all too late, recognised as the missing *Chesapeake*. Parker must have reported that the prospects of getting coal at St. John were nil, so they decided to make use of the pilot boat. On it they dumped Captain Willetts and all his crew and any bona fide passengers (except an engineer who was retained to 'assist' the Confederate crew) and the pilot landed them on Partuck Island, whence they went to Portland.

The chase was now well and truly on by six United States cruisers. The *Chesapeake*'s progress was watched from the shore and reported by U.S. officials and citizens. We get a report: 'The vessel then sailed in an easterly direction, subsequently it was seen alongside another vessel. It is supposed that he took aboard a supply of coal from her.'

Then followed many days of hide-and-seek up and down the Bay of Fundy and the more remote creeks of Nova Scotia. This game was already being played in grim earnest from the West Indies to the Carolinas and now, for the first time, there was excitement in the far North. I can, I think, best give you the flavour of this hunt by quoting from the *Diary of a Blockade Runner* written at the time.

> All signs of a ship are avoided. Anyone who showed an open light when we were near the fleet was liable to the penalty of death upon the spot; a cool, steady leadsman was stationed on each quarter to give the soundings; a staunch old quartermaster took the wheel and a kedge, bent to a stout hawser, was slung at each quarter. All lights were extinguished; the fire-room hatch covered over with a tarpaulin; and a hood fitted over the binnacle, with a small circular opening for the helmsman to see the compass through the aperture.

The look-out was the key man, and anyone who has ever had to peer through the gloom of a foggy day or dark night at sea will know what tricks one's eyes can play under these conditions. An alert man was essential, with good nerves, because a jittery watch-keeper with hallucinations would soon reduce the whole crew to a state of near panic. Of another trip the diary records,

> The cruisers are numerous and the little vessel is dodging back-wards and forwards all the forenoon—now going ahead till a column of smoke is seen on the horizon, now sheering and after a while resuming her old course. Once she has made a sighting, the Northern cruiser sends up a dense column of smoke to attract other vessels to her aid.

All through the December fogs and gales the chase went on. The biting winds and icy seas were bad enough but perhaps the most nerve-racking were the occasional cloudless skies or moon-light nights, when

The regular beat of our paddles through the smooth water sounded, to our ears, ominously loud. As we closely skirted the shore, the blockading vessels were plainly visible to us, some came so near to us that we saw, or fancied we saw, with our night glasses, the men on watch in their forecastles, but as we were inside of them all, and invisible against the background of the land, we passed beyond them undiscovered. The roar of the surf breaking upon the beach prevented the noise of our paddles from being heard.

And, presumably, the dark cliffs masked the smoke from the funnel.

Things on the *Chesapeake* were getting desperate, and soon there would be no more smoke because they had not been able to get enough coal from the captured brig to enable them to reach even Bermuda. However much Brain and Parker economised with the precious fuel, they could never dare let the boilers out as their only safety lay in speed, once they were spotted. The *Chesapeake* was unarmed and all the cruisers carried at least nine-inch smooth bores, and by then most of them had replaced those by seven-inch rifled guns, with a long carry and an accuracy out of all comparison to the old smooth bores.

Luck was not with them as no coal brig hove in sight, or only when too many cruisers were about. Having doubled back on their tracks to throw the hunt off the scent, past Freeport, round Yarmouth and Cape Sable Island, they used the last shovelfuls to creep into the then small and little-known port of Shelburne. Their luck changed and they found some coal—whether they took it by force of arms or whether the news of their doings simply had not reached Shelburne is not recorded. Nor do I know why they could not steam rapidly out to sea while the Federal cruisers were still busy searching the harbours of the Bay of Fundy. The coal may well have been bad or quite unsuitable or insufficient to carry them far enough south.

Indeed, this is confirmed when we get a despatch from Shelburne stating, 'They [the *Chesapeake*] left Shelburne on Dec. 13th with increased crew and 20 cauldron of coal [very little]. . . . She is supposed to be on the track of another coal vessel. A steamer was seen in Mabon Bay near Chester yesterday afternoon running about the islands.' She had left just in the nick of time, for we have another report. 'Tuesday. The *Ella and Annie* [a U.S. gunboat] arrived [at Shelburne] and coaled at 11½ am and then steamed out for her rendezvous at 3 pm. But the *Chesapeake* had already left at 9 am before. The *Ella and Annie* then turned back and steamed for Lunenberg, on orders which arrived in the evening.'

A day or so later the *Chesapeake* turned up in Le Havre River, flying the Confederate flag. This was important, because international rules say that if two ships from belligerent countries come into the same neutral port, a twenty-four hour gap must be allowed after the first ship leaves port before the second is allowed to follow; the assumption being that the *Chesapeake* would be regarded as a legitimately commissioned Confederate ship! Parker and Brain probably banked on the authorities in a remote Canadian port being a little vague about the small print.

Here Parker sold 'her cargo of provisions and liquors to the people on shore'. Now, I do not doubt this was becoming necessary to pay for the coal and, possibly, make more room below for extra coal for a long voyage; but with the possibility of capture hanging over their heads (with their dubious Letters of Marque) I would have thought this sale was highly unwise. International law states clearly that a privateer must take captured cargo to one of his own ports or, if unable to do so, destroy it. If it is sold elsewhere, the assumption is that it is for his own profit and he becomes, technically, a pirate. The fact that an authorised privateer would in any case draw a very handsome profit from the goods when sold in his own port is neither here nor there in the eyes of the law.

Parker's motives, however, appear to have been more than suspect, because 17 December finds the *Chesapeake* in Sambro harbour near Halifax with the Federal cruiser *Ella and Annie* not far behind.

The official history states simply, 'Parker and his party escaped to the shore', leaving Lieutenant Brain once more in command, presumably, to face the music and escape with or without the *Chesapeake* to the South if he could. Sambro, a hundred years ago, was a small village, at the head of a bay on the peninsula about fifteen sea miles from Halifax, where Brain went for provisions, and, one would agree with Brain, an excellent hide-out while provisioning for the voyage south.

However, the worst happened. The Federal gunboat *Ella and Annie* had received news of this and came in to find the *Chesapeake* anchored close by the British schooner *Investigator*. The crew member on watch, Wade by name, seems to have been arrested before he had time to alert the party ashore or to burn the *Chesapeake*. Perhaps he had instructions from Lieutenant Brain not to do so. I imagine they must have felt temporarily safe and with good hopes of eventually sailing the vessel into Wilmington, or she would have been destroyed earlier. Otherwise I cannot imagine why most of the crew had been allowed ashore in the search for provisions and coal. Under international law the U.S. gunboat was not allowed to fire on the *Chesapeake* while in neutral waters (within the three-mile limit) nor to interfere with her in any way or follow her out of harbour until twenty-four hours had elapsed. As it was, I presume no officials were on the spot and the gunboat's commander, Captain Nicholls, decided to take a chance and seize the *Chesapeake* in Brain's absence ashore. This nearly caused another international incident with the British Government, because not content with his first illegal action Nicholls started to tow the *Chesapeake* away. By this time there was intense activity ashore and the Canadian shore batteries were manned and waiting the command to open fire. The situation was only saved by the appearance of the *Dacotah*. An official report states: 'The *Ella and Annie* took the *Chesapeake* in tow and started for an American port but the *Dacotah* came up and ordered her into Halifax for adjudication by the British authorities.' Later, as the Confederate *History* states, 'Wade was aided to escape by a number of citizens who sympathised with the Southern Confederacy.' Whether Brain was similarly assisted by these citizens or arrested immediately in company of three of his crew who were named (Lieutenant Collins, seamen McKinnon and Seely) I do not know; but his name did not appear on the first reports which say several of the crew 'were arrested on warrants issued by a local magistrate who committed them for extradition on a charge of piracy'.

The scene moves to St. John, capital of New Brunswick, where the local papers really went to town. The *Gazette* reported—with more imagination than accuracy—

> St. John NB, Feb. 24—The police magistrate delivered judgment today in the *Chesapeake* case, ordering that the prisoners be committed to jail for surrender to the United States authorities. He said that the evidence for the prosecution discloses that the prisoners and other parties captured the steamship *Chesapeake*. It was the work of cowards and villains. It was piracy, robbery and murder. It was within the jurisdiction of the United States Courts, and a case within the Extradition Treaty. Application will be made for a writ of *habeas corpus*, so as to bring the case before the Supreme Court.

Even the Confederate *History* states, 'The affair gave rise to intense excitement.'

This was hardly overrating it, because by this time both Secretaries of State were in full cry, not to mention the British Government in the person of the High Commissioner. The United States, as the Federal States still called themselves, were demanding extradition on the grounds of a charge of piracy. The Canadian authorities were denying that there was a provable case for extradition and in any case stated that magistrates had no jurisdiction over charges of piracy. Mr. J. R. Benjamin, the Secretary of State for the Confederacy, was in the hot seat and, very understandably, playing it very cool. Firstly, he could not afford politically to antagonise a friendly Britain for the sake of defending a few naval personnel. They carried officially signed Letters of Marque but these did not cover operations inside neutral territorial waters. Secondly, the Secretary was much more interested in the vessel. But as it soon became clear that the British authorities were not going to uphold Brain's claim that she was a Confederate prize, and hence Confederate property, there was no option but to 'disavow the responsibility of his Government for the acts of Parker and Brain'. He added,

> That it was doubtful whether either Brain or Parr [his first lieutenant] was a Confederate citizen and that Brain had, in any

6

event, divested himself of the character of an officer engaged in legitimate warfare by selling portions of the cargo of the *Chesapeake* instead of navigating her to a Confederate port.

As a piece of logical government evidence in a court dealing with an international incident this was sheer moonshine. Not only was Brain being saddled with Parker's sale of goods, but if coal had been needed it could only have been bought with money. However, Brain had been warned before he started that if things went wrong, he could expect no official backing from the Confederate Government. So he could not have been surprised when the President announced: 'The Confederate Government will not demand the surrender to it of the men arrested by the provincial authorities, as their actual offence was "disobedience to her Majesty's proclamation and to the foreign enlistment law".' Meanwhile, the Union Government was still demanding blood, and appealed against decisions which denied them their pound of flesh. Much to Brain's relief, however,

> An appeal was taken to the Supreme Court of the province; and on March 10th, 1864, Judge Ritchie ordered their release on the grounds that no proper requisition had been made for their extradition; that piracy was not an extraditable offence; that a magistrate had no jurisdiction over piracy; and that the warrant was bad on its face.

While this was going on the future of the *Chesapeake* herself had been decided in the Admiralty Court at Halifax, with Judge Stuart presiding. The Confederate Government was represented (fortunately) by the Hon. J. P. Holcomb and the strong temptation of the Confederate Government to claim the *Chesapeake* as a prize (with all the ensuing complications and probable clamper on the release of the Confederate crew) was avoided, the *History* relates, by the frank avowal of Mr. Holcomb that:

> It is morally certain that the home government would not, under the circumstances, allow a claim for compensation for the surrender of the vessel by the judicial authorities and I cannot

but think that the presentation of such a claim by our government and its rejection—the case being one, as all must admit, very doubtful both in law and morals—would impair its public prestige and weaken the moral weight which might attach to its interpretation upon future and more important occasions.

So, by the end of January 1864, Judge Stuart had 'refused to consider the suggestion that the Confederate Government might make application for the vessel, the seizure of which might be declared to be piracy and so ordered her return to her owners'. This seemed to make everybody happy—or nearly so. Even Secretary of State Benjamin could write to the Canadian High Commissioner at the specific request of President Davis to say the President was 'much gratified that the superior judicial authorities of New Brunswick have rejected the pretensions of the Consul of the United States that the parties engaged in this capture should be surrendered under the Ashburton Treaty for trial by the courts of the U.S. on charges of piracy and murder'.

By now a distinct flavour of comic opera had begun to creep into what, at one time, had all the makings of a good honest international crisis. But there were ominous undertones that were not lost on Brain's small band of Confederates. The dismissal of the case for extradition by Judge Ritchie was quickly followed by the issue of new warrants for their arrest on the grounds that 'the offence of piracy was just as triable in the British Provinces as in the United States'.

Rather understandably, before the writs could be served the gentlemen to whom they were addressed had vanished into the desolate country beyond the Chiputneticook Lakes where the Provincial authorities would have little hope of finding, let alone apprehending them.

7

The Pony Express

A SURPRISE ATTACK ON THE GREAT LAKES

Long before things settled down in New Brunswick, Lieutenant
Brain and his crew were over the Adirondacks in deep snow and
pushing west through what had but recently been Indian country
to the Great Lakes. They were making for what was rather delightfully called the 'Pony Express'. This was the 'underground railway', as we should now call it, down which escaping Confederate
prisoners, including those from the big P.O.W. camps on Johnson's Island on Lake Erie, were piloted through enemy territory
on their way to rejoin the armed forces of the South.

The original Pony Express 'used to traverse the continent from
St. Louis to San Francisco'. It was organised by Major Picklin and
Colonel Finney who, with Captain Wilkinson, had led an expedition to the area a few months previously in a bid to free the
Confederate prisoners on Johnson's Island. News of the attempt
had been leaked to the Canadian authorities and it had to be abandoned at the last minute, but a few prisoners had escaped over the
ice to Sandusky in the gloom of a winter's night. It is of interest
to quote a few paragraphs from Captain Wilkinson's diary, because it shows very clearly what sort of 'state of alert' the shores
of Lake Erie had been put into just prior to Brain's arrival. It
makes Lieutenant Brain's subsequent action appear even more
hair-raising. Wilkinson states,

> It was arranged that our party should take passage on board one
> of the American lake steamers at a little port on the Welland
> Canal. We were disguised as immigrants to the West; our arms
> being shipped as mining tools; and when clear of the canal, we
> were to rise upon the crew, and make our way to Sandusky. As

the *Michigan* was anchored close to the main channel of the harbour, and we had provided ourselves with grapnels, it was believed that she could be carried by surprise. We had sent off our last 'Personal' to the *New York Herald*, informing our friends at Johnson's Island 'that the carriage would be at the door on or about the tenth'; our party had collected at the little port on the canal waiting for the steamer then nearly due, when a proclamation was issued by the Governor General, which fell among us like a thunderbolt. It was announced in this proclamation, that it had come to the knowledge of the Government that a hostile expedition was about to embark from the Canada shores, and the infliction of divers pains and penalties was threatened against all concerned in the violation of the neutrality laws. What was even more fatal to our hopes, we learned that His Excellency had notified the United States Government of our contemplated expedition.

The Wilkinson expedition wisely returned south without attempting an assault on either the steamer *Michigan* or the garrison of Johnson's Island but equally understandably, Brain, being much younger and less apt to bother himself about long odds, could not resist having a passing swipe at the U.S. commercial shipping on the Lake as he went through. As a matter of fact, the situation, in spite of the military precautions following the threat of Wilkinson's attack on Johnson's Island, was not entirely unfavourable to Confederate military action. Both the Canadian garrisons along the north coast of Lake Erie and the Union forces of the United States to the south were stretched pretty thin. Most important of all, the United States had, by treaty with Great Britain, only three gunboats to protect their trade with Canada across Lake Erie. This was a purely peace-time establishment and quite inadequate for policing a 240-mile-long lake if trouble started.

Trouble had started even before Brain and his men seized a small lake steamer, ran up the Confederate flag and had one glorious week of depredations on United States lake shipping, all with valuable cargoes vital to the war effort; but, again, all good things must come to an end and I remember reading in a subsequent letter, 'We were, unfortunately, forced to run her ashore and burn her to avoid capture.'

I imagine a gunboat must have run them to earth and started getting rough, and though it was not in Brain's nature to give up easily, he would have given a passing thought not only to the consequences of capture by Union authorities on the southern shore but also to the Canadian writ awaiting him if he ran the ship aground in the wrong place on the northern shore.

This venture must have been organised pretty well off the cuff and it can only have been a small steamer, as I can find no textbook confirmation of family records—nor can our kind friend Mr. Bronson, who lives on the spot and who did a recent search of contemporary Canadian newspapers for us. Brain may well have started something, because I have, thanks to Mr. Bronson, a long cutting from the *Free Press of London* (Canada) for Thursday morning, 22 September 1864, with the headlines:

THE STEAMER ISLAND QUEEN SEIZED AND PLUNDERED

She is scuttled and sunk

Statements of the Pilot, Fireman and Watchman

Our city and border was thrown into great excitement. The treacherous rebels who have been skulking along our border —the remnants of guerilla gangs and escaped prisoners of war from Johnson's Island and Camp Douglas, transported Kentucky secessionists and copper heads have organised piratical raids on our commerce. It has been a bold affair when we consider the small number known to be engaged and the audacity of its public management.

It is a great pity we have not time to quote more, because some of it is fascinating—such as the comment that when the ship was dredged up and brought into harbour,

She has been completely gutted, everything moveable including the piano was taken ashore by the pirates. She is also badly cut and defaced, a bad opening being made for the removal of the piano.

A nice touch if ever there was one, and almost, one might say, in the J. C. Brain tradition.

Before we return to him, I should make the point that all this was not just idle youthful adventure or even haphazard opportunism. The U.S. Secretary of State, William H. Seward, was by now getting really worried and regarded commerce raiding in this area, so far from the Southern battlefronts, as serious enough to invoke a clause in the Great Lakes' Treaty with Great Britain. He gave the statutory six months' notice that the U.S. Government was to increase its armaments on the Lakes. Even Edward Smith, who devotes only a dozen pages to the whole Civil War in his *England and America After Independence*, thinks the activity on the Great Lakes worth mentioning twice, one being 'The piratical seizure of a steamer on Lake Erie by a band of twenty men who went aboard as passengers, with one trunk of luggage between them, containing arms, hatchets, etc.'

To return to cousin Brain: you would have thought that with the hue and cry illuminated by the flames of a burning Federal steamship, he and his little party of Confederate officers and men would have been off down the Pony Express trail in a cloud of dust. But there was no dust. Instead we find him calmly going home to spend an evening with his mother at Box 623, Springfield, Ohio. This is a little county town a bit to the south of Lake Erie. She was, one imagines, getting a little worried by what she read in the local papers, including many hostile articles referring to the 'Piracy and Robbery' on the nearby lake. Following as it did so closely on the sight of her son John Clibbon's name in banner headlines across the front pages of the national dailies in connection with the chase and recapture of the *Chesapeake*, she must have been very pleased, and surprised, to see him in the flesh.

I expect he wanted to take her a few little presents, catch up with the family news from the old world and give her the most convincing proof of all—a personal visit—that at least he was not gracing the inside of a Canadian prison. There was a more poignant reason, I am afraid. His feckless father had, again, wandered off—

this time for good—and Brain would be making sure that she was provided for in a country torn by civil war; a war which had even split the Tabram family. She was not, of course, very far from her family, for while her son was fighting for the South, her brother Willam Gamble and his son (also christened John Clibbon just to confuse matters) were equally busy fighting for the North—though less enthusiastically, as we have seen.

Mrs. Brain's other consolation was that her daughter Lucy had married a John Hamilton and gone to live in Montreal, which was reasonably accessible by public transport. However, her son cannot have stayed long as his mother's house would have been among the first places to be searched. In any case, the Canadian border was rapidly becoming uncomfortable for footloose Confederate parties. Mr. Edward Smith cites another typical example of a party who, not unnaturally, got short of money and did what any sensible citizen would do. They went to the bank. I quote:

> They entered the town of St. Albans, robbed the three banks, and stole a sufficient number of horses to enable them to escape the more readily. Some of these men were pursued into Canadian territory and arrested but in the judicial proceedings that followed it was necessary to discharge them. The Confederate officers even protested against the breach of neutrality in daring to come after them; this was unfortunately right enough!

Episodes like these did not endear the Confederate bands to the Canadian authorities and the South was rapidly losing the sympathy it had enjoyed at the start of hostilities.

8

'Sail Ho—Right Astern, Sir, and in Chase'

THE COMMANDER STUDIES THE ART
OF BLOCKADE RUNNING

Down the Pony Express trail went Lieutenant Brain and his officers and men, because we next learn that by May he was back in the Confederate capital making his report to the Naval Headquarters and receiving instructions from the Secretary of the Navy Department, Mr. Secretary Mallory, for the future operations to which he and his crew were to be assigned. We gather this from one of his scrawly letters to my grandfather, to whom he writes, 'Dear Uncle Fred, . . . I could not find anything out when in Dixie about dear Papa. I was in Richmond all the month of May and was then ordered out with my officers and crew to capture this ship . . .'

This was written a few months later on the ship's notepaper of his next 'prize'—the S.S. *Roanoke*, a crack mail steamer of the New York and Virginia Navigation Company running under bond in the U.S. Federal Navy. Whether she had been hand-picked by the Confederate Navy Board as the fastest and most desirable ship suitable as a potential privateer, or whether she was selected by our Lieutenant (now Acting Commander) Brain, I cannot be sure. His letter seems to suggest the former. If so, they must have had considerable faith in the genius of this young man for pulling off the impossible because, being a relatively new, fast ship of 1,071 tons, she was on the Havana–New York run. This was one of the most heavily patrolled and blockaded areas of the whole coast, particularly as it was only 600 miles or so from the only two ports remaining in Southern hands—Wilmington and Charleston.

However, faith the Navy Board obviously had, and Brain and his crew must have given more than a passing thought to how this ship was to be added to the Confederate Navy. Time was running out. You had only to look out of the hotel window in Richmond, the Confederate capital, down Broad Street to the junction of 24th Street to St. John's white timbered church, to see the pinched faces of beggars and decent middle-class folk, whose farms had been devastated, trying to sell pathetic bits of domestic jewellery and household portables in exchange for food.

They were, of course, women; most of the menfolk had long since made a last appearance in the casualty lists or were simply listed as 'missing, believed dead'. True, you would see from time to time some well-dressed foreigners who were making a fat profit from blockade running; but they mostly stayed in the few remaining clubs which still kept open, rather apologetically, along 12th Street near the Confederate White House. Over the whole city lay the grey pall of disaster. The last great offensive was nearly a year old and the best of the last fully trained and equipped army of Northern Virginia had been buried under seemingly endless miles of green turf around the little college town of Gettysburg. The hospitals had run out of anaesthetics and medical supplies and had quite failed to cope with the remnants retreating back into Virginia to man the northern defences. Vicksburg had fallen in July and after the defeat at Chattanooga in November, Tennessee was lost and the way was open to Georgia itself and the last two vital ports through which supplies still filtered—at great cost in lives and ships.

While Brain was still in Richmond, news came in that Sherman was marching through Georgia to Atlanta in an encircling pincer movement with instructions 'to reduce that rich granary to a condition under which a crow flying across it would have to carry his own rations'. Sherman had 100,000 well-equipped fresh troops and though he was opposed by one of the ablest Confederate commanders, General Joseph E. Johnson, the Confederates only had 65,000 very tired men and could not give battle.

At sea the situation was no better. The most successful of the privateers, the *Alabama*, was at long last bottled up in Cherbourg, whence she was to sail out with flags flying in a few days' time to be shot to pieces by the crack armoured U.S. cruiser *Kearsage* which was waiting outside territorial waters. Her survivors were

picked up by the British yacht *Deerhound*, whose owner had also
sailed out so that 'his children should see the battle'! The *Nashville*
had been sunk and the *Florida, Sumter, Clarence,* and four or five
others had either been destroyed or forced to put into neutral
ports. Only the *Shenandoah* and *Chickamauga* were still afloat and in
commission. There was a desperate need for something spectacular, even if only to provide a moment's relief from the gloom, and
for the capture of some ship suitable to be armed to carry on the
war at sea. There was of course a fleet of efficient blockade runners,
but these were very small, fast vessels of a turtle shape mostly
built specially in England so as to be almost invisible against a
grey sea.[9] They ran bales of cotton[10] to Nassau or Havana and
munitions of war back in the other direction, dodging through
the thick blockade. They were only useful for this purpose and
certainly could not be armed and fitted out as commerce raiders.

The first thing Brain had to do was to get down with his men to
Wilmington, before the railway was cut by Sherman. There was
little rolling stock left intact and what there was was desperately
needed for moving munitions of war. If the capital Richmond had
been a grey city, Wilmington was complete chaos and a wilderness
of activity. Commander Brain even on the new pay of his acting
rank must have looked askance at the scene and at the civilian
adventurers who were making a profit out of the slaughter and
devastation of the war. But let me quote again from a contemporary account.

The harbour was crowded at times with lead coloured, short
masted rakish looking steamers; the streets alive with bustle
and activity during the daytime but swarming with drunken
revellers by night. Every nationality on earth, nearly, was represented there; the high wages ashore and afloat tempting adventurers of a baser sort and the prospect of enormous profits
offering equally strong inducements to capitalists of a specula-
tive turn. The monthly wages of a sailor on board a blockade
runner was $100 in gold and $50 in bounty at the end of a
successful trip; and this could be accomplished under favourable circumstances in seven days. The captains and pilots sometimes received as much as $5000 besides perquisites. It was

computed (so large were the gains) that the owner could afford to lose a vessel and a cargo after two successful voyages. Three or four steamers were wholly owned by the Confederate government, a few more in part and the balance were private property . . . but the captains and subordinate officers of the government steamers who belonged to the Confederate States navy and the pilots who were detailed from the army for this service, only received the pay in gold of their respective grades.

From all contemporary accounts, Brain would have found the old town of Wilmington unsavoury and distasteful.

Here resorted the speculators from all parts of the South to attend the weekly auctions of imported cargoes; and the town was infested with rogues and desperadoes who made a livelihood by robbery and murder. It was indeed unsafe to venture into the suburbs at night and even in daylight there were frequent conflicts in the public streets between the crews of the steamers in port and the soldiers stationed in the town, in which knives and pistols would be freely used and not infrequently a dead body would rise to the surface of the water in one of the docks with marks of violence upon it. The civil authorities were powerless to prevent crime *inter arma silent leges*. The agents and employees of the different blockade running companies lived in magnificent style paying a king's ransom (in Confederate money) for their household expenses and nearly monopolising the supplies from the country markets.

Indeed, by this period of the war, fresh provisions were almost beyond the resources of everybody. There are records of family servants newly arrived from the country of Virginia, who would sometimes return with an empty basket, having flatly refused to pay what they called 'such nonsense prices' for a bit of fresh beef or a handful of vegetables. It was recorded that a quarter of lamb sold for $100, a pound of tea for $500. Confederate money, which in the early part of the war had been nearly equal to specie in value, had declined catastrophically by September 1864.

Brain, however, would have been too busy to bother much

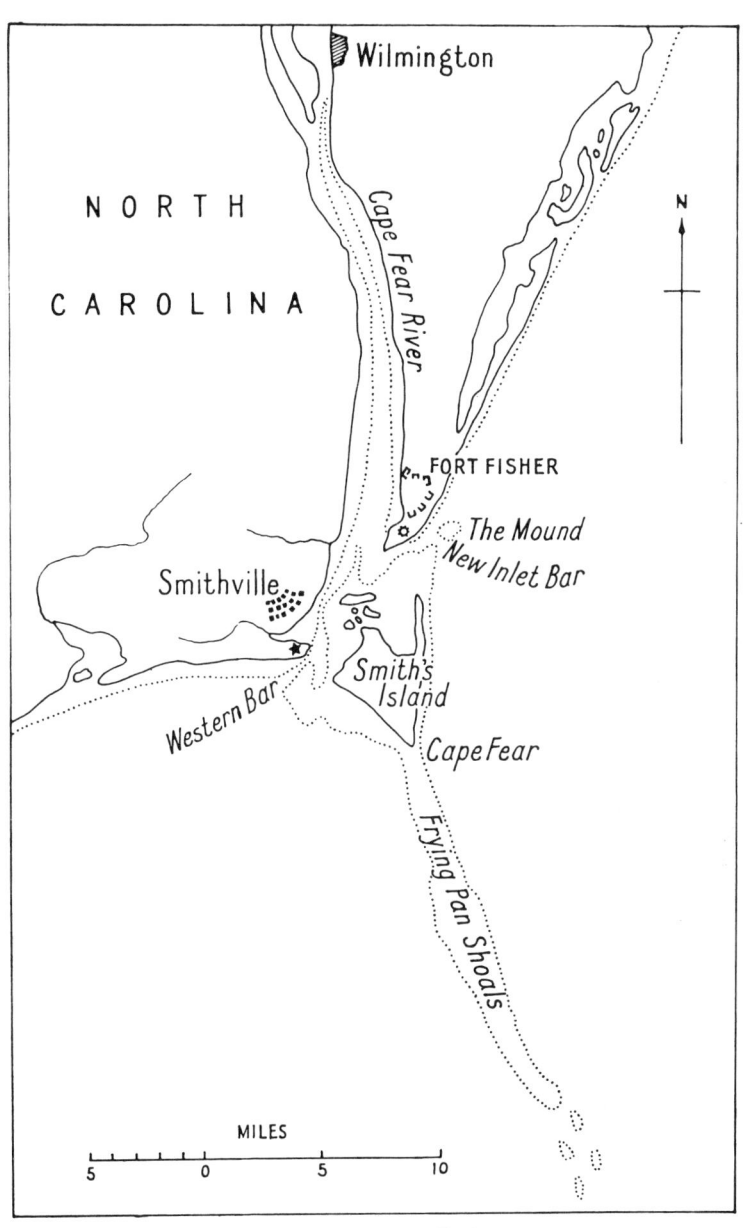

The approaches to Wilmington

about the general life of the town, for it was vital for him to learn as much as possible about the problems of running the blockade in preparation for his return journey. It would not have taken him long to discover the general layout of the harbour with its two entrances, one on each side of Smith's Island in the mouth of the broad Cape Fear River. From the river, the distance between the two channels is no more than a few miles. Thus an outward-bound blockade runner could drop down the river to Smithville and from this vantage point her captain could scrutinise the two Federal squadrons just beyond each of the two entrances and make his choice accordingly. For the blockading squadron it was not so easy to shift vessels quickly from off one bar to the other, for beyond the seaward side of the wedge-shaped Smith's Island were the Frying Pan Shoals, which enforced a long cruise out to sea before they could be rounded.

Brain would have learned that the light on Smith's Island which had been put out at the commencement of hostilities had been re-established and a structure had been built for a light on the Mound, the chief fortification of the headland by Cape Fear River. Captain Wilkinson had been charged with the duty of relighting these approaches to Cape Fear River and of detailing pilots and signal officers to the blockade runners. To provide the means for these lights every blockade runner had been required to bring in a barrel of sperm oil. Brain would have been briefed too about the 'range lights', which gave the pilot what a simple compass bearing would not give him: that is, an accurate line down various narrow channels. The range lights were only set after signals had been exchanged between an incoming blockade runner and the coastal batteries, or by arrangement with an outgoing vessel, and they were changed as circumstances required or the shoals altered.

Both inlets, Brain soon learned, had very nasty bars, but the shore was fairly steep-to, and in the dense shadow of compara-tively high bluffs one could ride to kedge and hawser very often without being seen by the blockading fleet against the dark shadow of the cliffs. The units of the blockading fleet, on the other hand, could often be seen from the decks of the Confederate blockade runners, steaming slowly on their beats a short distance outside. As soon as they were far enough away, a dash would be made for

Fort Fisher guarding the approaches to Wilmington, reproduced by courtesy of the National Maritime Museum

the bar. The point was that no blockading cruiser could get inshore of these small vessels and if the worst came to the worst the blockade runners could beach with the probability of being able to save most, if not the whole, of the cargo.

At Wilmington, however, the bar was not the only hazard. Two or three miles outside it there was an even more serious navigational danger, a sandspit called 'the lump'. There was good water either side of it but absolutely no way of knowing, on a pitch-black night, one's exact position in the passage, as distances from the shore were difficult to calculate accurately during darkness.

As Brain left Wilmington the news was not good. Owing to the constantly increasing vigil of the blockading fleet and the accession to the U.S. Navy of fast cruisers, many prizes had been captured of late. Their pilots were held as prisoners of war and the demand for those available for service increased in proportion to their diminished number, so that there was much competition between rival companies. They would of course have chosen a dark night to slip out and preferably one which was not too quiet because then the sound of the paddles could be heard for considerable distances by the Federal cruisers. At all other times it was drowned by the noise of the surf on the shore. Even with the best conditions, this run down the coast was not without its hazards quite apart from the blockading squadron. If a storm blew up, pilotage could become tricky and in thick weather the only thing to do was to find shallow enough water to anchor. With the surf thundering within a stone's throw on the port beam it was apt to be a little nerve-racking, especially in heavy rain storms, and all the regular pilots knew that the shore was so littered with wrecks that they could discover their position by sending a boat in to make a sketch of the wrecks and the angle at which they were lying. They were as good as any natural landmarks.

One of the most important natural phenomena on this coast, as any yachtsman will know, is the Gulf Stream and its effect on navigation. This would have been studied in extreme detail by Brain and his officers. It was the practice of every experienced captain of a blockade runner when making for port to cross the Stream early enough in the afternoon if possible to establish the ship's position by chronometer so as to escape the influence of that current on his dead reckoning. The lead always gave an indication of distance from the land though, of course, not of position. The current of the Gulf Stream varies in velocity (and within certain limits in direction at times) and under ordinary circumstances the Stream itself is almost as well defined as a river in its banks. The current is bent by natural phenomena such as strong gales but it is reasonably easy to calculate the direction and extent of the deflection. Local pilots would tell the captains that, in their opinion, the counter current inside the Gulf Stream was also influenced by prevailing winds. Wilkinson in his diary records that upon one occasion,

> While in command of the R. E. Lee we had experienced a very heavy thick weather and had crossed the Stream and struck soundings about mid-day. The weather then cleared so that we could obtain our altitude and near meridian. We found ourselves at least forty miles north of our supposed position near the shoals which extend in a Southerly direction off Cape Lookout. It would be more perilous to run out to sea than to continue our course. We had passed the offshore line of blockaders and the sky had become perfectly clear. I determined to personate a transport bound for Beaufort, which was in the possession of the United States forces and the coaling station of the fleet blockading Wilmington. Just as we were crossing through the ripple of shallow water off the 'tail of the shoals' we dipped our colours to a sloop of war which passed three or four miles to the south of us. This courtesy was promptly responded to. I have no doubt her captain thought we were slovenly and careless seamen to sail the shoals so closely.

So much did a passage depend on the time of crossing the Stream that Confederate navigators were unanimous in the opinion that the blockade would have been considerably more effective if the U.S. Navy had stationed a cordon of fast steamers ten or fifteen miles apart just inside the Gulf Stream rather than round the actual ports.

The cold north-westers were among the most dreaded winds for blockade runners, especially if they had to steam against a

7

strong gale the whole time and conduct a passage entirely by dead
reckoning because of overcast skies. The point was that, blowing
over the water of the Gulf Stream, the cold winds produced
clouds of vapour which would apparently 'rise like steam' and be
condensed by the cold wind into a fog so dense as to obscure every
object. As one contemporary skipper put it,

> At such times the skill and perseverance of the navigator would
> be taxed to the utmost. For instance, the sun, moon or North
> star caught through a sextant wet with spray and brought down
> to an almost uncertain horizon would furnish the only means
> of guidance where an error of a few miles in the calculations
> would probably prove fatal.

Very few blockade runners got through without receiving one
or more shots, but their profile made them difficult targets and it
was soon noticed that the shots were generally preceded by a flash
of calcium light or by some sort of blue light immediately followed by two rockets thrown in the direction of the blockade
runner. These signals would probably be concerted each day for
the ensuing night as they were constantly changed. Many blockade runners put to sea complete with a number of rockets smuggled in from New York and whenever all hands were called on
deck for the run through the blockading fleet, an officer was stationed on the bridge with the rockets. One or two minutes after
the pursuer had sent up his rockets the officer would be directed
to discharge his at right angles to the course in the hopes that it
would confuse the rest of the blockading fleet.

The best way, I think, of giving you the atmosphere of these
passages is to quote Wilkinson again:

> We passed safely through the blockading fleet of the New Inlet
> bar receiving no damage from the few shots fired at us and
> gained an offing from the coast of thirty miles by daylight. Very
> soon afterwards the vigilant look-out at the masthead called
> out 'Sail ho' and in reply to the whereaway from the deck rang
> out 'Right astern, Sir, and in chase'. The morning was very
> clear. Going to the mast head I could just discern the royal of

the chaser and before I left there, say in half an hour, the top-gallant sail showed above the horizon. By this time the sun had risen in a cloudless sky. It was evident our pursuer would be alongside of us by mid-day at the rate we were going. The first orders given were to throw overboard the deckload of cotton and to make more steam. The latter proved to be more easily given than executed, the chief engineer reporting that it was impossible to make steam with the wretched stuff filled with slate and dirt. A moderate breeze from the North East had been blowing ever since daylight and every stitch of canvas on board the square rigged steamer in our wake was drawing. We were steering East by South and it was clear that the chaser's advantage could only be neutralized either by bringing the *Lee* gradually head to wind or edging away to bring the wind aft. The former course would be running towards the land besides incurring the additional risk of being intercepted and captured by some of the inshore cruisers. I began to edge away therefore and in two or three hours enjoyed the satisfaction of seeing our pursuer clew up and furl his sails. The breeze was still blowing as fresh as in the morning but we were now running directly away from it and the cruiser was going literally as fast as the wind causing the sails to be rather a hindrance than a help but she was still gaining on us, and was fearfully close. We began to have visions of another residence at the Fort Warren, as I saw the big 'bone in the mouth' for she was near enough to us at one time to see distinctly the white curl of foam at her bows.

I wonder if they could have screwed another turn of speed out of her if they had known that the *Lee* had on board in addition to her cargo of cotton a large amount of gold shipped by the Confederate government!

There continued to be a very slight change in our relative positions until about six o'clock in the afternoon when the chief engineer again made his appearance. He came to report that the steam was running down. 'Keep her going till dark,' I replied, 'and we will give our pursuer the slip yet.' A heavy bank was lying along the horizon to the South and East and I saw a possible way of escape. At sunset the chaser was about four miles astern and gaining upon us. Calling two of my most reliable officers I stationed one of them in each wheel house with glasses directing them to let me know the instant they lost sight of the chaser in the growing darkness. At the same time I ordered the chief engineer to make as much black smoke as possible and to be in readiness to cut off the smoke by closing the dampers instantly when ordered. Twilight was soon succeeded by darkness. Both of the officers on the wheelhouse called out at the same moment 'We've lost sight of her' while a dense volume of smoke was steaming far in our wake. 'Close the dampers,' I called through the speaking tube and at the same time ordered the helm hard astarboard. I remained on deck an hour and then retired to my stateroom with a comfortable sense of security.

Everybody who had been on the run had his own stories of being shot at and having got away. By and large most boats got through as long as they were commanded by experienced hands.[11] Very often they never saw the cruisers that fired at them, especially if the cruiser was inshore and against a dark line of coast. In any case, the average blockade runner, once clear of places like the Frying Pan Shoals where blockading cruisers were always stationed, was almost invisible at night like harlequin in the pantomime. Nothing showed above the low turtle deck except two short masts and the smoke stack, which was very often led horizontally so that it could discharge into the sea.

The nonchalance with which many of the passengers, especially military ones, took the normal shelling is summed up as well as anywhere in another quotation from Wilkinson.

The colonel who had seen service in the army of Northern Virginia was sitting upon the wheelhouse when the first shot was fired and calmly remarked (to no one in particular) 'That is pretty firing'. At the second, 'That is *very* pretty firing'. And when the third shell burst upon the deck he jumped upon his feet and exclaimed with much emphasis, 'If that isn't the prettiest firing that I ever saw I wish I may be damned!'

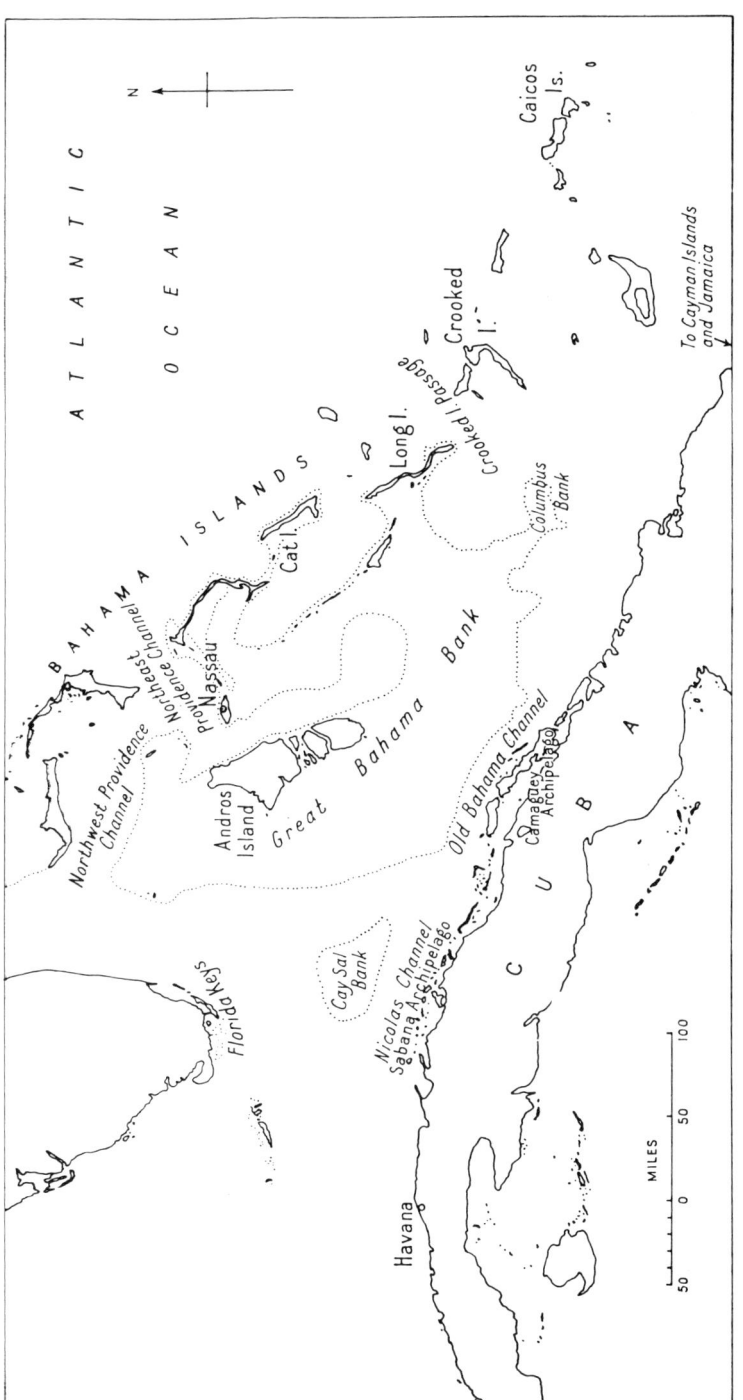

Chart showing the navigational hazards from the Bahamas to Cuba

Anyway, after four days and nights Brain's ship would be approaching Nassau, the capital of New Providence, with a harbour conveniently tucked away between Paradise Island and the mainland. Now I do suggest you turn to page 89 and study the drawing or rough chart of the Bahama Islands there because, as I well remember from sailing there, it is one of the most tricky bits of navigation, even if you have not got a hostile force of cruisers waiting for you at every turn. In places over the Great Bahama Banks you can go for a whole day with only a level fathom or certainly no more than one or two fathoms under you, and Nassau itself lies in the middle of shoals with only the North-East Providence Channel to the east. The North-West Providence Channel is the normal entrance from the Gulf Stream and below it (and of very great interest to blockade runners when the main channels were too stiff with cruisers) is the Tongue of Ocean. This is a long channel of deep water running right down into the Bahama Banks themselves but with no way out except over the shallows. Very often the blockade runners had only a foot or two under them and could only tackle this in very calm weather.

The normal run for mail steamers like the *Roanoke* would be up the Gulf Stream between the Bahamas and the Florida Keys. Brain must have realised from the very beginning that this would not be possible for a Confederate prize because he would not know the daily passwords or signals that would be expected as routine between a mail steamer on a regular run and the blockading U.S. cruisers. He must have seen from the charts that his only chance of making a get away from Havana would be to hug the Cuban shore, down the Old Bahama Channel and then make his way between the islands, probably through Crooked Island passage between Long Key and Long Island where there would be sufficient depth of water. Equally important would be a study of the banks and shoals between the Islands in case he was headed off and hard pressed. His visit to Nassau would be extremely important for this reason, and although he would have had to put into Nassau in any case before going on to his ultimate destination, Havana, it would have been time well spent. One skipper has left a record which I quote to give you the flavour of a similar operation.

In order to economise in coal and to lessen the risk of capture I determined to approach Nassau by the 'Tongue of Ocean', a deep indentation in the sea bounded on the South by the Bahama Banks; and to reach the 'Tongue' it was necessary to cross the whole extent of the banks from Elbow Key Lighthouse. On arriving off the lighthouse we were disappointed in our hope of finding a pilot and no alternative was left but to attempt the transit without one, as we had not a sufficient supply of coal to enable us to pursue any other course. Our chart showed 12 feet of water all over that portion of the banks and the *Giraffe* was drawing 11 feet. But the innumerable black dots on the charts showed where the dangerous coral heads were nearly awash. On the other hand we knew there could be no swell in such an expanse of shallow water. So, waving adieu to the keeper of the lighthouse, we pointed the *Giraffe's* bow to the banks which showed ahead of us, smooth as a lake and almost milk white. It was early in the morning when we started and the distance to be run to the Tongue was only 60 or 70 miles. Taking my station in the fore rigging I could easily direct the helmsman how to avoid these treacherous black spots. It was the Florida Reef all over again and my experience in surveying the coast stood us in good stead here. We were so fortunate indeed as to never once touch the bottom, although the lead frequently showed less than 12 feet and about three o'clock in the afternoon the welcome blue water showed itself ahead. It would have been impossible to make the transit in cloudy weather but the day was fortunately clear. Occasionally when a 'trade' cloud would approach the sun, we would slow down or stop, until it had passed when the black patches would again be visible. The iron plates of the *Giraffe* would have been pierced as completely as if made of pasteboard if she had come in contact, even at low water, with those jagged coral heads. Before dark we were out of danger and next morning came to anchor in the harbour of Nassau.

That, I think, shows very vividly the pilotage rather than navigational problems of approaching Nassau by the back door, when the main channels were too effectively blockaded.

I suppose Nassau must have been the busiest place in the whole West Indies during the Civil War. It was through this port that practically all the supplies of hardware (which was a euphemistic name for munitions of war), food, clothing, and other products including gun mountings and metal parts were ferried to the Southern States. At Nassau they were transhipped from British, French, or European ships to blockade runners, many of which were of course owned by British skippers who were running them as a speculation. Havana was also busy, but it was three or four hundred miles further away and, in addition, there were considerably fewer channels, creeks, and possibilities of approach, because Havana opens directly on to the Straits of Florida and was very much more difficult to leave unobserved.

Nassau must have been an extraordinary sight with the light draught, low, hump-backed blockade runners jostling with U.S. cruisers and local commercial and fishing boats in port. The blockade runners carried Bahama Bank pilots, who knew every channel. For some reason, the U.S. cruisers seemed not to have Bank pilots and, as they drew more water, were compelled to keep to the open sea. Occasionally one of them would heave-to outside the harbour and send a boat in to get the latest news from the American Consul and then go back to its cruising ground off the Abaco Light or whatever its station was.

There in Nassau Commander Brain would be able to get plots of all the channels through the reefs and shoals, though, at that time I doubt whether they would have been as fully and accurately buoyed as they were thirty years ago when I knew them. The distance from Charleston is about five hundred miles and from Wilmington about five hundred and fifty. But at Sandy Point at least one squadron of U.S. cruisers had its base—an important element in calculating the course.

9

'The Passengers Were Not a Little Surprised'

THE FAST MAIL STEAMER *ROANOKE* IS THE NEXT TARGET

How long Brain and his small party of officers and men were in Nassau, I do not know. Nor do we know how he shipped from that port to Havana. All we know is that he spent at least a few days in Nassau before moving on. The party were in Havana by the end of August and made a thorough reconnaissance of both the port and the habits of its officials. The nearby channels and outlying islands of the Archipillago de Sabana would be studied from charts. There would be one advantage, in that the Spanish authorities in Cuba were far less strict on protocol than the British in Nassau. This might, of course, cut both ways.

It was perhaps unfortunate that the *Florida*, the only Confederate privateer afloat at that precise time, was known to be in the area. The *Alabama* had just been sunk off Cherbourg, and the *Tallahassee*, *Olustee*, and *Shenandoah* had not yet set out on their belated raiding cruises. Admiral Dahlgren, the Union Commander in Chief, South Atlantic, had alerted all officials and captains of U.S. cruisers in the blockading squadrons to double lookouts and to have gun crews at the ready. That was the luck of the game, and at least the *Roanoke* could not be mistaken for the *Florida* even on a dark night. All the same, it highlights the sheer audacity of Brain's attempt on the *Roanoke*. The *Florida* had first become famous when Captain Maffitt sailed her right through the assembled U.S. Federal fleet, then blockading Mobile (near St. Louis on the Mississippi), in broad daylight without sustaining any crippling damage. This sort of thing was not encouraged, as a

93

The *Florida* (a famous Confederate privateer)

privateer's main duty was to destroy the enemy's commerce and avoid conclusions with more heavily armed naval units. I mention it, however, to give some idea of the resolution of her captain and hence the flutter among blockading cruisers—especially as Captain Preble commanding the Mobile fleet had subsequently been court-martialled for not sinking the *Florida*.

Captain Maffitt has left an amusing account of the scene on the *Florida* after one of their more sumptuous captures:

> The *Florida*'s deck, when the crew were at their meals, was a curious scene; the plain fare of the sailors being served in costly china, captured from the homeward bound 'Indiamen' and the scamps had become fastidious in their taste about tea. I had the pleasure to carry into Wilmington ten or twelve chests of the finest hyson, which were distributed among the hospitals; and a lot of silver ingots made a narrow escape from confiscation.

The law officers in Bermuda, whom Maffitt had consulted, had assured him that they would be adjudged legal prizes of war in the British courts, and so they were shipped to England, instead of the Confederacy, and there returned to the claimants.

In Havana, as elsewhere in neutral ports which had accorded belligerent rights to the Confederate Government, the Confederate naval cruisers and blockade runners were admitted into harbour on equal terms with the United States men-of-war. There was, of course, no exchange of civilities between the officers of ships of the rival navies, but the ordinary sailors seem to have had no such inhibitions and, from a contemporary account, generally 'got drunk together ashore with mutual good will. A Jack Tar is probably the only representative left of the old "Free Lance", who served under any flag where he was sure of pay and booty. The blue jackets will fight under any colors where there is a fair prospect of adventure and prize money'. This, though written by a Confederate ship's captain, applied equally at that date to both navies.

When Brain and his party got to Havana two U.S. naval cruisers were in harbour, nestling against the quay with a number of sleek, grey, rakish-looking Confederate blockade runners happily rubbing shoulders with them. The Spanish government officials, from the governor downwards, were making too much easy money to do more than observe the essential minimum of international neutrality laws.

Brain would have wasted no time in studying the charts, especially those showing the bars and sandbanks along the north Cuban shore, also noting what lights and sea marks had been left in operation for the benefit of the blockading cruisers. As I have already said, the *Roanoke*'s regular run straight up the Gulf Stream along the Florida Channel would be impossible due to the hue and cry, and because of the presence of the *Florida* Brain knew every ship in the main channels would be checked and questioned en route for any sightings. Even if he captured the code flags and passwords he could not possibly defend his ship in an emergency with small arms only and a crew of five against a well-armed naval cruiser. Besides, there would be the regular crew of about 50 to guard, together with 70-odd passengers.

So, if you turn to your chart on page 89 you will see why he eventually decided upon the dangerous coast of Cuba through the Nicolas Channel, between the coral reefs of Cay Sal Bank and the archipelagos of Sabana and Camaguey. Once down the old Bahama Channel, he would be able to cut round Cape Verde and squeeze between the South Point of Long Island and Crooked Island up the Crooked Island Passage—hoping none of the U.S. cruisers would dare to follow, or be patrolling such a dangerous and ill-marked passage.

There is no record of where Commander Brain and his officers and men stayed, but in a neutral port with a great number of both Confederate and U.S. vessels in the harbour (in addition to those on patrol outside) everybody was able to lodge and go about their official or unofficial business as they pleased—until they tried to put to sea, when things began to happen.

Each side had its agents and official resident consuls watching every move of crews and ships loading, and passing daily predictions to the offshore cruiser captains of likely departures of blockade runners. Many a Spanish official was receiving both United States and Confederate pay at the same time. Wilkinson's diary gives the flavour:

Away to sea in the offing is a large United States cruiser with steam up, watching the proceedings. She is just outside Spanish territorial waters and is waiting like a spider for the next fly; the fly has other ideas. As it grows dark a boat puts off to the Federal cruiser from the United States Consul, who keeps a vigilant eye on all that goes on, to say what ship is likely to put out during the night. The sun sets, the short tropical twilight is over and dark shapes, showing no lights, begin to creep out, keeping in territorial waters and each having good pilots for the Bahama Banks.

Indeed, by the last week of September the atmosphere must have been very tense. The *Roanoke* was due in from New York on the 26th and was scheduled to sail again on the 29th. There was one significant stroke of luck. She was due to sail at about 1630 hours. This would be ideal for Brain as it would give the Confederate party darkness to overpower the crew and give the blockading cruisers the slip—at least temporarily, enough for a head start. True, it would also mean negotiating dangerous and unfamiliar channels in the dark, but that was a risk that had to be accepted.

One other event must have added to the tense atmosphere prevailing among Brain's small party at that moment—that is, apart from the rapidly deteriorating situation at home, where the land forces, now surrounded on all sides, were being relentlessly pushed back onto their capital. Immediately after the sinking of the *Alabama* on 19 June, a message was sent from the Confederate Secretary Mallory primarily to Commander Bullock, Naval Agent in the U.K., ordering him 'to replace the *Alabama*, at any cost, with some craft whether it were suitable to that service or not'. News of this would have reached Commander Brain also and no one knew better than he did that, with only the *Florida* left afloat as a commerce raider, the need was desperate.

Perhaps this is a suitable point at which to explain the attributes of a 'suitable' vessel for commerce raiding. Firstly, she had to carry a good spread of sail because, once outside routes used by steamships and hence supplied with coaling bases, sail constituted the only reliable means of keeping at sea for any worthwhile length of time. This must have been one reason for picking out the *Roanoke*, as she carried more than the average area of canvas for her size, 1,071 tons.

Steam power was of course vital for coastal work such as blockade running where the competition was from fast enemy cruisers capable of steaming in a calm and adding screw or paddle wheels to sail power in a chase. One trouble was that, in proportion as the Confederate States appeared to be losing the war, so the neutrals were tightening their regulations as to mechanical overhauling and the provision of coaling facilities. For instance, the *Florida* had recently been refused a second coaling in the area because she had just coaled at a nearby port. After the *Chesapeake* incident, no one knew better than Brain the disadvantages of the merchant steamer entirely dependent on coal when cruising long distances.

On the other hand the *Roanoke* would undoubtedly make a good gun platform. She was almost exactly the same size and build as the U.S.S. *Kearsage* which had just sunk the Confederate privateer *Alabama*. The *Kearsage* carried seven guns, throwing a broadside of 430 pounds, including two 11-inch rifled pivot guns which decided the action, Brain would have noted. The rest were smooth bores throwing 32- or 62-pound shot respectively. Brain must have known that there were some British made rifled guns of 11-inch calibre to be had in Bermuda. Also the *Shenandoah*, a vessel Bullock had his eye on, was to mount, besides two little pop guns on the poop deck carried by all merchantmen, three rifled 32s on each side and four 8-inch shell guns.

The *Roanoke*, built of white oak and brigantine-rigged (a most flexible arrangement), was a suitable choice structurally. She had iron knees, beams, and frame, with a fine lined wooden hull, planked from keel to gunwale in teak. Her iron masts, bowsprit, wire rigging, and steel yards would carry her canvas in anything short of a full blow. She had the latest type of side wheels and her speed through the water under engine alone was a good twelve knots—faster than most opposing cruisers. Her engines were relatively new. She measured 218 by 32 feet and drew 10 feet 6 inches.

Punctually on 26 September, in the late afternoon, the anxious watchers saw their intended prey steam slowly into port, accompanied by the cruiser *Juniper* which was based at Havana. The *Rhode Island*, Brain had noted, was also in port coaling. He now had two and a half days in which to finalise his plans and make a note of the crew and, by tactful questioning in shoreside taverns, get to know how they were armed and as much as possible about the lay-out and position of cargo and passengers. Crew routine and signalling procedure would also be vital. We do not know whether or not Brain was able to get aboard and look round in disguise. I suspect this was also managed somehow.

Brain found she carried a crew of 50, of whom the officers and non-commissioned ranks wore arms permanently. The remainder were supplied from the armoury as occasion demanded. He had only three officers (Parr, Little, and a purser, Lathrope), two engineers and four seamen, all from the Southern States, to effect the capture of the vessel and deal with the captured crew and 40 or 50 passengers, should he succeed. The odds. could not have looked exactly promising!

Subsequently, we notice a nice touch: he acquired and included in his baggage 51 pairs of handcuffs—not 50, but one spare, just in case!

Ironically, the Master was one Francis A. Drew who, in the balmy days of peace, began his sea-going career in Virginia and whose first command was none other than the little *Jamestown* which, as you will remember, was later to provide the first nautical experience for trooper Brain and eventually his escape from uncongenial army life. Furthermore, Brain's chief engineer had actually served pre-war in the *Jamestown* under Captain Drew as it turned out in evidence at the subsequent court-martial in New York.

By now, on the bustling water front of Havana it is midday and there is the usual flurry of last-minute stores being swung aboard. The coaling of the mail steamship has been completed and the crew are taking leave of their girl friends as sailors do the world over. Brain has managed to get some of his crew on board as ordinary passengers, complete with passports, visas, and officially stamped documents—but not all! Their luggage, if opened, would somewhat surprise the captain, containing as it does arms and

The M.S. *Roanoke* (the second prize), reproduced by courtesy of the National Maritime Museum

ammunition in addition to the 51 pairs of handcuffs. The list states there are '24 cabin passengers and 16 in the steerage'; and one of the cabin passengers is a dark, handsome man called Mr. Johnson, who will be familiar to you.

At the initial official enquiry, held subsequently in New York, there was some discrepancy of evidence as to how the remainder came aboard. Mr. Nichols, the first officer, stated, 'The vessel stopped three different times and took on others, who came in boats. First, one man was taken, then a boat with two, and another with three men. These passengers were strangers. No passengers were ever received before in that way.' Mr. Nichols thought they could have come on board in boats only for the purpose of avoiding application to the British Consul. He added that, 'No hesitation was manifested by the Captain to take the men on board, the purser saying they were all right.'

The matter was cleared up finally when Captain Drew himself wrote a personal letter to the *New York Times*, defending himself against public questions in that newspaper. He stated,

Many readers are doubtless under the impression that passengers are landed and received at Havana.

That is not so, all merchant (and mail) steamers pass the city and anchor three quarters of a mile beyond the Harbour and passengers employ what are known as 'shore boats' to take them to the city. On the 29th of September (1864) I was hailed half way there and about a quarter of a mile from the city, by two boats with passengers having both tickets from our office and regular passports which Mr. F. E. Bawley my Purser assured me were duly visa'd by the American Consul—including Mr Johnson's—I being on the upper deck at the time.

I have often done this and so have other Havana steamers.

Then he goes on to explain that though he had had no special warning about this trip, he and all captains had been several times warned about possible attempts 'to capture the Havana–New York steamer'! He had taken all precautions, especially as to arming all the officers and some of the crew.

Anyhow, picked up Brain's party was, and the *Roanoke*

proceeded on her way at her full speed of 12 knots. Besides her 40 passengers and 50 crew, she was carrying $4,000 in gold, $17,000 in greenbacks, and 215 boxes of sugar, besides cotton and, as one can imagine, a large number of boxes of Havana cigars for the New York gentry.

For what happened in the next few hours we have rather too much conflicting evidence. This includes contemporary newspaper cuttings such as a letter by a passenger, dated 10 October to *The Times* in England, and an account in the *New York Times*, dated 4 November, of the subsequent examination of the original officers and crew of the vessel by the official 'collector of New York', as he was called. This includes long statements by First Officer Nichols, Chief Engineer Higgins, and the steward, Mr. Cook—all trying to justify their actions at the time. The best account of the capture is, I think, the letter by an English passenger to the London *Times*, so I shall quote it.

THE CAPTURE OF THE UNITED STATES' MAIL STEAMER ROANOKE.

TO THE EDITOR OF THE TIMES.

Sir,—On the 29th of September the United States' mail steamship Roanoke, Francis A. Drew, Master, left the port of Havannah, bound for New York, passing the Moro Castle at 5 p.m., with 24 cabin passengers, and 16 in the steerage, the officers and crew numbering 50, making 90 persons on board. The steamer proceeded on her voyage at a speed of some 12 knots per hour, running within sight of and a short distance from the coast during some two or three hours, the time passing agreeably and without anything unusual having occurred until about 9 20 p.m., when, about 25 miles off the coast of Cuba, the passengers were not a little surprised at hearing proclaimed, by a man dressed in the Confederate naval uniform, who proved to be no less a personage than the capturor of the Chesapeake—viz., Lieutenant John C. Brain, and who in a loud voice said, "In the name of the Confederate States of America I demand the surrender of this vessel as a lawful prize," and calling upon Captain Drew to surrender as a prisoner of war. The announcement was immediately followed by the discharge of several pistols, with which the attacking party were armed. From that moment the work of capture commenced. Lieutenant Brain, taking the upper deck of the vessel, accompanied by officer Little, the purser, and a seaman, secured the captain and officers on that deck, placing them in irons, while officer Parr, the first and second engineers, and three seamen proceeded with the officers and crew on the main deck, until Lieutenant Brain and officer Little, leaving the upper deck in charge of the purser and a seaman, went below to the assistance of officer Parr, when at 15 minutes past 10 o'clock, in the space of 55 minutes, the capture had been consummated, and the vessel was proceeding on her voyage as the Confederate States' Prize Steamship Roanoke.

There was but little violent resistance made, except by the carpenter of the vessel, who, after surrendering, seized an axe and aimed a blow at the head of officer Parr, but the axe falling short of its mark four balls pierced the body of the man, from the effect of which he fell and expired in a few minutes.

In a short time after the capture Captain Drew was released upon his parole.

Having been favoured with a perusal of the register of the Roanoke, I learn from it that she was built in New York by the New York and Virginia Navigation Company, who were her sole owners ; her dimensions being in length 218ft.; breadth, 32ft.; dept, 10ft. 6in., and measuring 1,071 tons. Also, from a certificate attached to her register, it appears that the vessel was seized at the port of New York under the Confiscation Act of the United States, and released on bond.

Lieutenant Brain exhibited to me his orders and commis. sion from the Secretary of the Navy of the Confederate States to make the capture of the Roanoke. Whether the fact of her having been owned by the Navigation Company aforesaid, some of the members being citizens of the Confederate States, and on whose account she was seized, as above stated, thus dispossessing said citizens of their property, caused the Government to order her capture, I am not advised. It would not, however, require any extraordinary stretch of the imagination to enable one to arrive at that conclusion.

The following are the names and residences of the officers and crew who made the capture of the Roanoke :—John C. Brain, acting master, Holly Springs, Missouri ; H. A. Parr, master's mate, Nashville, Tennessee ; Thomas R. Little, master's mate, Mobile, Alabama ; Alexander Lathrop, purser, Kentucky ; Robert Troth, first engineer, New Orleans ; James Conlen, second engineer, Galveston, Texas ; Robert Gage, seaman, Mobile, Alabama ; Arthur Morehead, seaman, Louisiana ; H. J. Braddock, seaman, Union Town, Kentucky ; J. D. Van Amburg, seaman, Staunton, Virginia.

Lieutenant Brain informed me that on his arrival off St. George's it was his intention to provision and coal the vessel, parole and land the passengers, officers, and crew, and take the vessel to Wilmington.

Letter to *The Times*, England, from a passenger aboard the *Roanoke* at the time of capture

The list of names and addresses of all the Confederate officers and men seems to have been displayed on the notice board for the benefit of the passengers.

Once again, both the planning and execution of the assault must have been pretty efficient to have achieved complete surprise on all four decks with an almost total lack of casualties. It might easily have been a particularly bloody business, as there is evidence that Captain Drew and his officers had drawn their revolvers but were given no time to use them effectively. The first officer explained later that two of the Confederates had 'leaned' on him and told him if he opened his mouth they would 'blow his brains out'. He was invited to surrender to the Confederate States of America and given one minute to decide. He answered, 'In that case I had better surrender.' He was put in irons. The captain, who had retired to his cabin at 1750 hours leaving the first officer in charge of the watch, 'appeared with his pistol cocked but was unable to see where to fire because of the dark'. The only casualty was the carpenter who, having surrendered and then thought better of it, had only himself to blame.

However, the main task had only just begun. The waters between Havana and New York were stiff with enemy cruisers and the first problem of the new acting commander of the *Roanoke* was to give them the slip. The non-appearance of the vessel would be quickly reported and he must have turned 180° back to the Cuban shore. Thence he skirted along the dangerous passage of the Nicolas Channel below the Cay Sal Bank, down the Old Bahama Channel, with eighty miles of shallow reefs on the port side and the jagged Camagüey archipelago to starboard. Daylight would find them, he hoped, off the Columbus Bank and at least not expected by any roving cruisers until he had made his way out to sea through the little-used Crooked Island Channel. It must have been a hair-raising passage—and luck seems to have been with them.

Once clear of the Great Banks and Islands he could relax and complete the organisation of his new command which had already been begun by his first officer Lieutenant Parr. After half an hour he offered Captain Drew freedom on parole, which was accepted. It was also offered to and accepted by a number of officers, who, after the initial shock, preferred freedom to remaining in irons.

The Confederate flag had by now been run up and a notice of Confederate rates of pay had been meticulously drawn up by the new purser and pinned on the notice board in the mess room and crew's quarters. About thirty preferred to remain firmly in irons, thinking, no doubt, of the court-martial which might await them should they ever get back to the Northern States in one piece. But fourteen, including a number of firemen and coal passers, signed on as temporary seamen in the Confederate Navy—and why not? The money was good, better than their Federal rate of pay. They were paid a month's wages in advance, from the commencement of the new regime.

The rates laid down by Brain were $60 for firemen and $50 for coal passers. There is another nice touch. They were all paid in good United States currency (not depreciated Confederate notes) and, as on another occasion, it was taken straight from the safes in the purser's office.

The steward, Mr. Cook, seems to have been a bit uncooperative. He said at the subsequent enquiry, 'Brain told me the *Roanoke* was going to Wilmington (after dropping the passengers at Bermuda) and that she needed a steward and would have to keep me. Brain promised me a hundred dollars down and a hundred dollars a month until the *Roanoke* should get to Wilmington.' Mr. Cook made much at the enquiry of the fact that he declined the offer. A compromise was reached however, in that he was left unfettered by day to carry on his normal duties on behalf of the passengers and especially, one imagines, to the satisfaction of the new captain and his officers who had become very partial to good food and wine during the last two months.

Indeed, after the near-starvation situation in the Southern States, the good living in both Nassau and Havana must have seemed something akin to heaven for any Confederate visitor. We know, also, that Brain was by this time very partial to a good cigar and now he could indulge his whim with the best the Cuban planters could produce.

As to the passengers, how were they taking this change of management? As indicated by the *Times* correspondent quoted above, they seem to have been in no way incommoded and to have taken the whole proceedings rather calmly. Their gossip round the bar had been temporarily interrupted by the shooting and general 'noises off' or perhaps the next course at dinner had been a little late in arriving but, apparently they were soon fraternising happily with the new officers of the watch in their strange uniforms. The Confederate flag had been spread out in the saloon until such time, on the second day, as it had been thought fit to wear it defiantly at the after ensign staff. The only point that was clear to all was that they were now on a sort of mystery cruise with one fact certain, that they were most unlikely to dock in New York as originally scheduled.

As darkness fell on the third day of the *Roanoke*'s career as a unit of the Confederate Navy, her acting commander could hope to be clear of the coral reefs and shoals of the Bahama Islands. A slightly reduced speed of 11 knots, husbanding the precious coal, would mean just over 260 sea miles in 24 hours, give or take the influence of tidal currents and head winds. She would not be very manoeuvrable under sail alone in restricted waters, so steam power would certainly have been used until, after about two and a half to three days, they would if not stopped by blockading cruisers be in the open Atlantic.

Brain now had to decide on his next course of action. Rightly, he ruled out a direct dart for Wilmington. He had enough coal aboard for the attempt but, we must remember, only nine officers and men to run the ship and control 36 actively hostile enemy seamen and 14 suspect recruits. In addition to this, 30 passengers would make resistance to an armed boarding party from any cruiser that caught up with them extremely difficult.

So, having given up any thoughts of a direct attempt on Wilmington under such conditions, he laid a course for Bermuda, the nearest neutral port. This was only about 200 miles (one day's steaming) further away than either of the two ports remaining in Confederate hands. It had many advantages. He would be able to land the passengers, who would be within easy reach of New York by regular steamships, and he could coal ship with any luck. Furthermore, he could also land the *Roanoke*'s former crew members and recruit a Confederate crew from among the 'paid-off' seamen of blockade runners that had come to grief in one way or another. Even guns might be available, if the Confederate Consul was worth his salt and could organise a suitable entrepreneur. Brain now had the right money to pay for them, in acceptable United States greenbacks or, better still, gold if necessary— though that would be worth more to the Southern Government if it could be brought back intact.

We don't know how far he had been able to brief himself on the incidence of blockading United States cruisers outside the three-mile international limit, or alternatively, whether the British authorities' views of neutrality were hardening against the South because she was obviously and rapidly losing the war. Once in, he might not be allowed to leave, until a lengthy court case had settled the 'prize' status of his ship.

Anyway, here he was, in the Atlantic on the fourth day, having given all the cruisers of Admiral Larchner's West Indies squadron the slip and navigated his ship successfully through 600 miles of the Bahama Islands with their outlying coral reefs. He marks the occasion characteristically, not by a party—though I do not doubt a few toasts were drunk—but by sitting down and writing one of his enchanting, misspelt, scrawly letters to my grandfather: written, of course, on the ship's notepaper with a little engraving of his newly acquired ship at the head of the paper—so charming that I have had parts of it reproduced for you on p. 108.

This letter, I think you will agree, reveals the most engaging side of this contradictory character. Primarily he was a 'loner' and an individualist who, in a modern war, would have been a natural for commando raids. Many a young man in the Tabram family records had had a wanderlust deep down. With John Clibbon, it was a driving force. He was already acquiring a reputation for turning up in the most unexpected places and returning to base as casually as if nothing much had happened. As a boy, he had had an urge to find out how things worked and to get behind the façade of the marble temples of authoritarian society. He was never so happy as when turning the world upside down to do it. He was, at twenty-five, already becoming a legend in the little villages of the Southern States and the taverns where tired men met to forget the gloom of constant defeat and approaching starvation. His achievements may seem inconsiderable to us when viewed down the long avenue of the years, but at the time, against

Confederate States
Prize Steam Ship Roanoke.
at Sea Oct 4th 1864

Dear Uncle Fred
I trust that you will excuse my negligence and neglect of you I can assure you it was not

because I did not think of you. I should be ungrateful indeed if I did so for you were all very kind to me when I was last at Nailsworth. (Then follows family matters of no general interest and an account of the action, virtually as above.) The ship and cargo will be worth about £100,000 in the Confederacy. I will post this letter in Bermuda where I call for coals and a pilot and sail for Wilmington N.C. My kindest love

to yourself aunt C. dear Grandma and Grand Papa and all of the little ones I have sent you a Trophy for the Office
I Remain your Affectionate Nephew
Master C.S.N. Jno Brain Acting Comdr C.S. Prize Roa[noke]

Letter from Acting Commander Brain C.S.N. to his Uncle Fred, written on the *Roanoke*'s notepaper

the black clouds of defeat they appeared as the last ray of sunshine in an otherwise drab world. So his health was drunk and hastily composed ballads about 'Bold Captain Brain' were beginning to be sung round the camp fires on winter nights.

Backwoodsmen in the North still discussed over drinks in the log cabin the madcap Southerner who dropped in one night from a blazing wreck with a cheerful 'hi there', cleaned them out at backgammon or crown and anchor and disappeared into the night as unaccountably as he had come. I have even seen the stern Victorian countenance of my aunt soften into a reflective grin at the mention of his name. This was about as near smiling as she ever got.

There was nothing physically spectacular about him but he must have had some sort of personal magnetism that attracted men and kept them loyal under trying circumstances. We know he was an ebullient and amusing companion who lived life to the full with few regrets—they were, unfortunately left for other people. I think also that the uncertainties of war made him cling even more firmly, as his letters show, to those moments in his past, all too few perhaps, which were real and stable and reflected the cosy side of life. Mostly they led back to his grandfather's house, the Bannut Tree House at Nailsworth, which, with its memories of family Christmas parties with the lights ablaze in the mullioned windows, seemed to exude a stability and was the sort of home he had never had in the wandering life with his own parents.

This is why, when he was exhilarated or despondent, we find him writing as then to his Uncle Frederick and showing us the naturally affectionate and engaging side of his nature which always had the female members of the community on his side, whatever boyish escapades he had recently been up to. 'Aunt C' in the letter was my grandmother, Charlotte Lewis, and the aunt already mentioned was one of the 'little ones'—probably, at the age of twelve, avidly reading about his doings in the letters to *The Times* as well as in the cuttings from the American and Canadian papers which were sent back to the old country by the Bristol cousins in the North.

Incidentally, I find the 'Trophy for the office' rather a pleasant touch, especially in the middle of a somewhat desperate venture. I am afraid history does not relate what it was going to be because, as far as I know it never reached England—for reasons which soon become only too clear.

The *Roanoke* seems to have had a trouble-free run out into the Atlantic, for the next thing we hear is that by 7 October they are safely off St. George's, Bermuda. The winds must have been unkind and contrary because the coal situation is beginning to cause the new captain a certain amount of anxiety. The sixty-four dollar question was whether to enter a neutral port and claim the rights of a recognised belligerent or whether to heave-to outside the three-mile limit and retain absolute freedom of movement and organise all necessary transhipments by tender. In the event it had to be played by ear, according to the disposition of any United States cruisers that were found on patrol in the area.

Brain already had certain information as to what to expect. His brother officer Captain Wilkinson had reported:

During the month of March, 1863, the *Lee*'s port of destination was St. George's, Bermuda. This island is easily accessible on the southern side, and was much resorted to by blockade-runners. Surrounded on all the other sides by dangerous coral reefs, which extend for many miles into deep water, a vessel of heavy draft can approach from the south within a cable's length of the shore. A light of the first class at the west end of the group composing the 'Bermudas', is visible for many miles in clear weather. It may as well be mentioned here, that the blockade-runners rarely approached *any* head land during daylight; 'preferring darkness rather than light.' The agent of the Confederate Government, Major Walker, with his staff of assistants, lived at St George's; and he and his accomplished wife always welcomed their compatriots with genuine hospitality. The house of Mr. Black (an assistant to the Major) was also open to us, and no sick exile from home will ever forget the tender nursing of Mrs. Black and the kindness of that whole family.

Confederate privateer and U.S. naval cruiser share the anchorage—St. George's, Bermuda, reproduced by courtesy of West Point Museum

He had also reported that when in command of the *Chickamauga*, he had not been allowed to enter the harbour, 'until after a correspondence, in which I stated the fact that our engines needed repairs; but we lay outside twenty-four hours before even this permission was given'.

This was due to representations of the resident United States Consul. At first he was even forbidden to coal ship and then only to take in a supply 'sufficient to carry the *Chickamauga* to the nearest Confederate port'. This was in spite of the authorities being informed that the vessel was properly commissioned and was then on a cruise. Wilkinson had stated that in his view, 'the Governor had no right to enquire into the antecedents of the *Chickamauga*, or to question the title by which she was held by the Confederate Government'.

But, as he adds wistfully, the fortunes of the Confederacy were now waning, and this was the year before the capture of the *Roanoke*, so Brain would have given the 1864 situation some painful thought. The deciding factor must have been that all foreign powers had by now more or less agreed (even taking into consideration the fact that the two remaining Confederate ports were so closely blockaded as to make it impossible to take prizes in for adjudication) on a prohibition 'of the sending of captured vessels into their ports'.

The only ray of sunshine in the situation was that the United States blockade commander, a typical sea dog if there ever was one, called Admiral Wilkes,[12] had just had a blazing row with the authorities, partly owing to the boarding of a British mail steamer off the north coast by St. Catherine's Point and partly due to his insistence on stationing cruisers on permanent watch in Five Fathom Hole. The Governor had reminded him equally firmly that it was forbidden to 'anchor in the Fairway' and that the *Tiogo* 'having filled her bunkers and store room at Bermuda, was not eligible to remain in or return to those waters for three months'.

Another U.S. ship, the *Sonoma*, having arrived with plenty of coal but expended it cruising off the port, was not entitled to replenish it as that was in violation of 'the spirit' of the ruling.

In the circumstances, it is not surprising that Brain decided to heave to outside territorial limits and make a signal for a pilot.

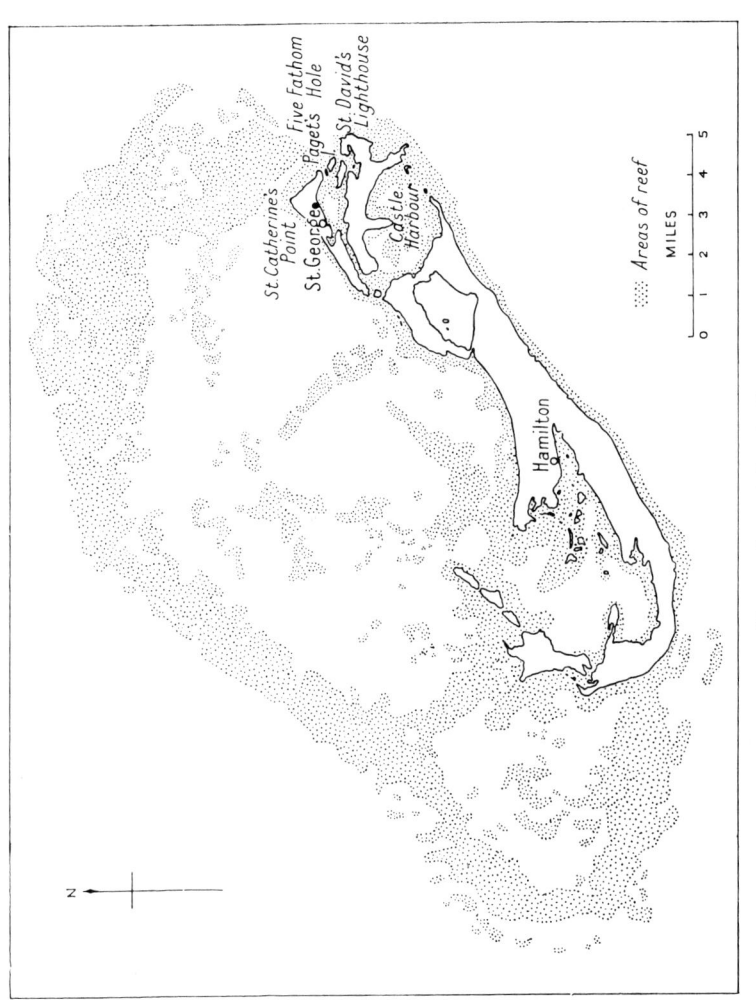

St. Catherine's Point
Five Fathom Hole
Fagets Hole
St. George
St. David's Lighthouse
Castle Harbour
Hamilton

Areas of reef

MILES
0 1 2 3 4 5

N

Bermuda and its reefs

On arrival, the pilot took the vessel to Five Fathom Hole where she was anchored, and Commander Brain went ashore with him for a quick reconnaissance and a consultation with the Confederate agent, Major Walker. His first officer, Lieutenant Parr, had strict instructions to maintain a head of steam and be prepared to leave if a U.S. cruiser hove in sight. They had been lucky so far in that the heat seemed to be off for the moment, as there were no signs of enemy ships outside the harbour.

But there were other signs; signs in the sky of high, windy mares' tails that reinforced a suspicion that one of the dreaded north-east gales was about to burst upon them from the frozen wastes of the New England mountains. It had been brewing for twenty-four hours and now it was touch and go whether they would beat it and get the coal aboard in time and the passengers and their belongings ashore before conditions became impossible, particularly as the U.S. crew could not be turned loose in Bermuda to petition the authorities before Commander Brain had completed his negotiations. One thing was becoming clear. Unless the sea moderated he would have to forego acquiring guns for the ship, even guns in packing cases that could have been mounted in Wilmington when he got through the blockade.

Nevertheless, having posted his letter to the Bannut Tree House, either the charm and ingenuity of Brain or the string-pulling of Major Walker and his assistant, Mr. Black, worked the miracle, because by the next day, 8 October, a coal brig was on its way out to the waiting *Roanoke*, now cruising again outside territorial limits. According to another account, she had not been idle, but had filled in the time capturing two other brigs, one being the *Village Girl*. There was still no sign of the enemy cruisers but the sea, which had been just lumpy before, was getting uncomfortably rough and the sky had more than a hint of line squalls and was looking like a Wagnerian backcloth of impending disaster. Even the 'persuaded' ex-Federal members of the crew seemed to have caught something of the urgency and worked with a will, at least from habit if nothing else, at transferring the coal from the brig to the *Roanoke*'s bunkers. It was becoming increasingly difficult and dangerous work. The trouble was that steam had to be kept up all the time in case enemy cruisers were sighted, as sail alone would not be enough to effect an escape. By then it was also necessary to have the paddles turning slowly in order to keep 'hove-to'.

As night fell, the last sight must have been of that infernal brig 'standing on her beam ends, now one way, now another'. As one of the captured firemen remarked at the subsequent enquiry in New York, 'There was so much sea on, that we couldn't get the coal aboard faster than we had to burn it, as we had to keep steam up all the time.'

Brain now has to turn his attention very seriously to a more immediate and human problem. He is responsible for the safety and lives of thirty passengers—among them a number of ladies—who are, understandably, getting a little restive. Most of them must have been as sick as cats, because there is nothing more stomach-shifting than lying hove-to, rolling in the trough of each Atlantic wave and now and then taking it green over the bow. They have my sympathy, because the *Roanoke* was built for speed and as her dimensions were a bit 'narrow-gutted' she must have rolled abominably.

This explains why the captain transferred his passengers at first light, at the ungodly hour of 4 a.m. on 9 October, to the *Mathilde*, one of the captured brigs, and sent them into harbour to escape the impending gale. There is a somewhat unctuous statement made by First Officer Nicholas later, at the enquiry in New York, to the effect that 'The ladies would not leave the vessel unless I would take charge of the boat [brig] as some of the Confederate officers had been drinking.'

Well, between you, me, and the gate post, as the saying is, I would not be surprised, as everybody had been having a very trying time and the prospect looked even blacker.

The ex-officers and crew of the *Roanoke* were also released and allowed to go ashore in the brig along with the passengers. Even the firemen and coal passers were released from their 'contracts' with the Confederate Government because Brain, or the Consul, had managed to recruit forty-seven rather more willing Southern sailors who had been rounded up from the St. George's wharves the day before and were even now on their way out to the *Roanoke*.

They were, on arrival, immediately set to work on the bucking coal brig to try and transfer at least enough coal to see the vessel safely across to Wilmington. But the squalls were rapidly becoming more frequent and increasingly severe. They managed to get 15 tons transferred but this was burned as fast as they got it aboard and things were beginning to look desperate. They could of course have sailed the vessel across the Atlantic to Wilmington but would have been an easy prey, without power from the engines, for the first armed cruiser they met and the *Roanoke* was not provisioned or provided with navigational aids for a long voyage to the old world or even some South American country where arms and provisions might be purchased.

The gale was now upon them with the full fury of the north-easter. There is evidence (from subsequent statements) that they had burned their last ton of coal aboard and coaling from the brig had had to be abandoned as hopeless until the weather moderated —which it showed no signs of doing. Brain took the only possible decision under the circumstances to prevent his ship's recapture by the United States authorities and ensure the safety of his officers and men. He transferred the gold, some of the cotton and cigars (apart from those distributed to the crew members) to the bucking brig along with most of the crew—no mean feat in itself. Then he and Lieutenant Parr set fire to the *Roanoke* and managed to get aboard the brig themselves and sail her rather reluctantly one must suppose, into St. George's, Bermuda.

On whichever side of the war one's sympathies lie, I think it must be agreed that the gale was a rather undeserved and vicious stroke of ill fortune. Brain had carried out his almost impossible orders from the Navy Board and achieved the desired ship, sailed her safely to a neutral port from where he had managed to get both coal and a loyal Southern crew and then had to abandon her at the eleventh hour, merely because blind fate, in the shape of the elements had stepped in to prevent his transferring the coal to the ship's bunkers. Incidentally, it highlighted the Achilles heel of these hermaphrodite ships of the period which were poor performers under sail alone and, without very numerous coaling stations, were apt to be without steam because of the inefficiency of the early type of boiler.

The sight of a ship on fire at sea is always a disturbing, if not terrifying sight, even if one's personal emotions are not involved. In this case both a fine ship and Brain's early hopes of sailing her into Wilmington were blazing to heaven against the black storm clouds, with the flames streaming out across the shadowy water with its white-crested waves in the gale-force wind. It must have been a tragic sight to any young man's eyes as the Confederates scudded under storm canvas towards the land—a sad end to Brain's second noteworthy prize. His only consolation was that a prize court conducted with British impartiality was going to be preferable to another dose of mainland justice in a United States already confident of a rapidly growing sense of approaching victory. In the growing darkness and guided by St. David's lighthouse beacon they squeezed in past Paget's Island to the sheltered harbour waters.

Ashore, there was complete chaos and the whole waterfront was not unnaturally in an uproar. Some of the population of the old town of St. George's were on the hilltops watching the last blazing throes of the *Roanoke* while others were busy plying the released seamen with drinks in return for accounts of their adventures. Captain Drew and his purser were closeted with the British Governor demanding the arrest of the 'pirates' and their extradition to the Northern States.

The cotton bales, boxes of cigars and other such valuables as had been salvaged from the mail steamer were landed and put under guard in a warehouse. The Confederate commander and his crew were first interrogated by an embarrassed constable at Five Fathom Hole, after which they were lodged in the famous Hotel de Boggs to await official notification of any action the British authorities might decide to take when they had digested and discussed all the available evidence.

Meanwhile the forty-seven newly recruited Confederate crew members whose tour of duty had been somewhat brief and unrewarding, apart from their having been given their month's pay in advance, were celebrating with all the other Southern sympathisers in the waterside taverns and drinking places along the shore. Ballads were being improvised on the spot and sung to rollicking popular tunes. Just to show they still had their tails up in spite of everything, I give you one of them as a sample. This was jotted down by local reporters and printed as a broadsheet by the *Bermuda Mirror* on its own presses.[13] I think I should remind readers looking at this and other halting and unscannable drinking songs that, before condemning them at their face value as rubbish, one has to remember they were very much like modern West Indian calypsos, put together on the spot as they were sung—in this case by the forty-seven local recruits.

A good tune like 'Langford Gaol' (for this one) and plenty of drink would make them sound much better!

The official enquiry dragged on for three days and while the Southern sympathisers drank and sang, the Northerners raved and went about muttering darkly about 'mock trials' and the mortal threat of piracy on the high seas going unchecked. The governor and his legal advisers seem to have been in no doubt from the beginning that there was little they could do but release the Confederates. There was the official document embodying the Confederate Government's commission to a naval officer, Commander Brain, and indeed each of his officers and crew men were specifically mentioned by name. The document duly bore the signatures of the Secretary of the Navy, the Hon. Stephen Russell Mallory and Secretary of State, the Hon. Judah P. Benjamin, and the seal of the Confederacy.

Britain had recognised both governments officially as belligerents, with full belligerent rights. Brain had not contravened any of the port regulations and had remained outside territorial limits. What the warring navies liked to do on the high seas were their own affairs. So Brain and his crew were, once more, free men—much to the rage and frustration of the Union officials in general and Captain Drew in particular. It is a small island, St. George's, and I do not think I dare even try to picture their emotions, seeing that every time they wanted a quiet noggin they would be deafened by patriotic Southern choruses emanating from every other open window and floating down the street on the evening air.

The salvaged goods were more of a problem and they had to await a formal prize court. But the cigars! They were a different matter. The trouble was that there was a British government duty

SONG OF THE ROANOKE.

TUNE.—*Langford Gaol.*

On the sixth day of October, in Eighteen sixty-four,
We shipped in Bermuda, and sailed from the shore,
In search of a steamer, of which we only knew,
That to take her to Dixie we were the chosen crew.

That night we found the steamer, the Roanoke by name,
Commanded by bold Captain Brain and his gallant men,
Who took her from the Yankees, as she left the Cuban shore,
On the twenty-ninth September, in eighteen sixty-four.

In the harbour of Havanna, these Confederates paid their fare,
For a passage to New York, with no intention to go there,
But to take the vessel as a prize, as they did with many more,
And parole the prisoners, and send them all on shore.

Her crew they mustered forty-eight, officers and men,
They were nearly five to one, the Confederates were but ten,
But being ready for the job, they took them by surprise,
And were in full possession, ere the sun did rise.

Bold Brain he made some purchases, from the captured crew,
Of Sugar and Cigars, with Chronometer or two.
He paid each person for his share in Chase's currency,
For a Southerner always respects man's private property.

In the offing of Bermuda, the prisoners were paroled,
And boats to carry them on shore from the Roanoke were lowered.
Off went the prisoners and passengers, the latter twenty-five,
The former giving praise to God they'd got on shore alive.

Our Captain then concluded to abandon his former plan,
There were strong suspicions 'gainst a boy from Wilmington.
He set fire to the prize, and we pulled our boats to shore,
And now the steam-ship Roanoke's gone the way of many more.

The captors and the prize crew were arrested on that day,
By some one's orders who had Yankee government pay.
"I am sorry," said each constable, " but my duty I must do,"
"So come to the Hotel de Boggs, you're one of the pirate crew."

We were brought up for the trial, the three ensuing days,
Charged with the crime of piracy, committed on the seas.
Our Captain shewed Commission, the Crown withdrew the charge,
The prisoners were acquitted, and now they roam at large.

But now, thanks to Providence, our trial it is o'er,
And on the broad Atlantic we will roam again once more.
To burn up Yankee vessels, we will never fail,
So farewell to Bermuda, and St. Georges Gaol.

To Captain Brain and Officers we tender our thanks,
For the cigars they gave us which they bought from the Yanks.
And although we were willing on them duty to pay,
John Bull pounced upon them and took them all away.

Now I think it is high time to finish up my song,
And state though tried for piracy we still did nothing wrong.
Then three cheers for those Confederates, repeat them far and near,
I hope they'll burn more Yankee ships, if Abe dont end the war.

Printed at the Office of the " Bermuda Mirror."

on cigars imported from the West Indies and Brain had forgotten to pay it—it was deemed. He readily offered to pay duty, not only on those remaining in the warehouse, but on those already consumed by his men ashore: but his offer was not good enough. Solemnly, with all the panoply of local officialdom and without, one gathers, a hint of a smile, they were condemned to confiscation on the grounds that 'They had been smuggled in, in an attempt to evade duty'.

One cannot escape the conclusion that the British are a wonderful nation. Who but they would have thought that one up? A crack mail steamship had just been burned to the water in full view of the whole island, the township was littered with forty-nine very sore, angry United States naval personnel, and thirty disgruntled passengers who had paid for a fast passage to New York, not to mention bales of doubtful wet cotton and a hoard of gold—but justice had been done, in full, as far as the cigars were concerned!

Loose in the Atlantic

BRAIN CAPTURES THE *ST. MARY'S*

Back in what was left of Virginia and the Carolinas, the war was nearing its inevitable end. Famine was rife and only General Lee's gallant army of Northern Virginia stood between the loss of the capital, Richmond, and defeat. Sherman had cut them off from all help from and communication with the Mississippi and the West. The last two ports, Wilmington and Charleston, were already threatened with capture by land if not sea.

There are some who would agree, at this point, that our John Clibbon Brain and his crew had done their bit and might without undue censure have remained with a comfortable grandstand view of the death throes of the Confederacy, from a safe distance across the waters of the Atlantic Ocean. But, to his credit, Brain does not seem to have had any hesitation. I cannot feel that he had any desperate personal feelings for his adopted country but, not unlike a more famous character, Walter Scott's Dugal Dalgetty, he seems to have had a simple loyalty to his paymasters. He was wearing the uniform of the Confederate States and that was that, until he was released by events.

So back he went with the next ship to run the blockade and back with him went his little party of nine buddies to report to naval headquarters in Richmond—if they could get there. They found the capital greatly changed for the worse, even since early June when Brain had last been there. The few cavalry horses left were suffering badly from malnutrition and three greatly superior, well-fed, and well-armed armies were closing in on the capital. True, the Northerners' forces had also suffered enormous casualties, but they could easily replace them. There was no possibility of replacing the Confederate casualties—even the old men and the boys had been used up. There was virtually no transport left.

There were plenty of senior naval officers to man the Navy Board, but no seamen to man the remaining ships now bottled up in the shallow upper reaches of the James River.

The new year dawned bleakly across the Rappahanock and passed unnoticed down the deserted streets of Richmond to the waterfront where, apparently, our commander had been sent to rejoin what was left of the James River squadron. The squadron was composed of the flagship *Virginia* and two other ironclads, the *Richmond* and the *Fredericksburg*, gunboat *Drewry*, torpedo boat *Torpedo* and torpedo launches *Scorpion*, *Wasp*, and *Hornet*. They were all firmly confined to the shallow upper reaches by a boom, a greatly superior Northern naval force, and massive enemy batteries.

One hope remained. If the squadron could achieve complete surprise one dark night, fight its way down and destroy the U.S. fleet at City Point, it might, by some miracle, capture and destroy General Grant's main supply base from which he was investing the last Confederate stronghold of Richmond. Anyway, it was better than scuttling without fight, and this would have to be done as soon as Richmond fell.

Flag Officer Mitchell had been chafing for many months at the enforced inactivity and so had many officers besides Brain, who at least had had a good run for his money elsewhere. I have been unable to find out in which ship he was serving. He would not have stood any chance of a command as there were far too many regular (ex-U.S.) naval officers waiting for any vacancy in the few remaining ships. In any case the authorities would be regarding this young man with a certain amount of embarrassed frigidity at the moment, as there was no doubt about his having, however unjustifiably in official eyes, become a popular hero in the eyes of the despondent populace. They were still busy singing his praises in village inns and round any camp fires, in extempore and gusty though illiterate ballads. Here are a few verses of one more that I have in the original printing, as an example of the sort of thing that was sung.

THREE CHEERS FOR BOLD BRAIN

Three cheers for bold Brain and his gallant crew,
We will sail with bold Brain the world through and through.
Bold Brain's commission is to burn and destroy
All United States vessels that he can decoy.

Chorus Huzza! huzza! for bold Brain so true,
We will sail with bold Brain the world through and through.

To Havana they went with a small crowd of boys,
For to capture the Roanoke without making a noise,
On board they did go with cool looks as you see
And at nine that same night there was a bit of a spree.

Chorus Huzza! huzza!

They came to Bermuda but coals could not get—
They set fire to and burned her—says Brain, 'Boys, don't fret!'
On Sunday they landed on Bermudian shore,
And were soon introduced to the Station House door.

They washed and they dressed and refreshment was had,
With a coat for a pillow and the floor for a bed.
The people in crowds stood gazing about
When they found that the Roanoke had gone up the spout.

Captain Brain was alarmed by the ring of a bell,
And was then introduced to 'Boggs' Hotel',
For two or three days they were all drilled about,
But all they could say, 'She has gone up the spout!'

All this cannot have endeared a young amateur sailor of 26 to orthodox martinets of senior officers and I cannot help hazarding a shrewd guess that the consensus of opinion 'upstairs' was that 'the sooner the young gentleman starts on his travels again the better for all at Headquarters'. The war could then be lost (as was inevitable anyway) with dignity and without any unseemly frivolity on their part. This, I am sure, was the attitude of Rear Admiral Semmes who took over on 18 February and immediately reintroduced the same rigid naval discipline for which he had been noted when in command of the *Alabama*. By that time Brain, with at least the tacit permission of the Board, if not a formal directive, had already disappeared into the blue again together with his crew in search of further prey.

But first we must record the last naval action in which he took part as a serving officer posted to a squadron. It was a fiasco from start to finish. A high spring tide had been chosen, since it would give the heavy ironclads sufficient water in which to float. Also it was known that many of the United States ironclads had been withdrawn for the attack on Wilmington (which indeed fell on 18 January)[14]. Because of this, there appeared to the authorities to be at least a forlorn hope of success. A directive was issued to commanders to the effect that any ships which succeeded in breaking out would attempt to make their way into the Pacific and join the *Shenandoah*[15] which was then operating off San Francisco, California. The river at that time of the year was a sheet of broken ice, dotted with miniature icebergs from the thaw higher up, and was known to be sown liberally with anchored torpedoes in the lower reaches.

The squadron passed successfully under two enemy batteries without being spotted, the sensible pickets being all under cover round fires in their rifle pits, out of the blistering wind and snow flurries. The ships were safely brought to anchor short of the boom defences which, the report states, 'were set adrift with a few licks of a cold chisel at the anchored end of the spar'.

Captain Mitchell then took the *Fredericksburg*, the ironclad with the shallowest draught, through the boom defences and returned in a boat for the *Virginia* and the *Richmond*. So far, so good. But on his return he found they had both anchored too near the north bank and were firmly aground. They were soon targets for scorching and accurate fire from the batteries all along the southern shore. The Confederate squadron was very undermanned by inexperienced seamen and tired army recruits who had been hastily collected for the attempt and it says much for the leadership of the naval officers that there was no panic, especially as by 9 o'clock the U.S. ironclad *Onondaga* had been brought up and was firing into them at point blank range with her two 15-inch guns. Being grounded, they could not reply as the enemy ship could easily manoeuvre into a position where neither Confederate could bring her fixed guns to bear through the narrow ports. The *Drewry* and the *Wasp* were soon sunk and the *Virginia's* armour pierced, killing 6 and wounding 14. Even so, the *Fredericksburg* was recalled, the two ironclads were eventually refloated and the depleted squadron retreated up river to await final self-destruction when Richmond fell on 2 April.

Long before that happened, Commander Brain and his small crew of faithfuls were again on a 'lone wolf' prowl. I imagine he saw no future in sitting around and waiting for the inevitable cataclysm. According to the *Confederate Veteran* of 1896, he had been wounded in the engagement, having been hit in the head by a bullet or a piece of shrapnel which left him 'with a prominent scar on his left forehead'. But in any case, after the last abortive attempt of the James River squadron it must have been painfully clear that there was nothing a young naval officer could do in the tiny tract of land then left to the Confederates, except provide another mouth to eat precious food. So, when we next hear of him, he was again deep in the heart of enemy territory and not far from the capital, Washington itself.

On 1 April, this quite irrepressible young man, scar and all, bobs up off the mouth of the Patuxent River in the Chesapeake, just north of the Potomac which runs up to Washington. We get our first news of him when the U.S.S. *Galena* berths at Delaware Breakwater, Lewis, on 3 April. Her commander, Lieutenant Commander C. H. Wells, sends a despatch post-haste to the Hon. Gideon Welles, U.S. Secretary of the Navy, Washington City[16]. He reports that Brain has captured a yawl and is loose among the Northern shipping in the Chesapeake.

Mr. Secretary Welles immediately (7 April) forwarded the despatch to Commander Parker commanding the U.S. Potomac flotilla. But, by the time this despatch (which went on to enumerate other ships captured by the Confederates under Commander Brain) was received it was many days out of date. The Union authorities on the spot must have had the news some days before, and Parker's reserve cruisers would already have been sent full steam in pursuit, hoping to intercept Brain before he gets clear away into the Atlantic, where he will be much more difficult to locate and bring to action.

After 31 March, things happened fast. Brain has only, so far, a relatively slow yawl, probably only armed with portable guns and small arms and he is in a very restricted inland waterway, stiff with enemy cruisers. To do any major damage to U.S. shipping, it is imperative to find and seize a fast ocean-going ship already armed by the enemy and provisioned for extended cruising. So, at 1 o'clock on the morning of 1 April (perhaps a not inappropriate date!) he boards and captures the *St. Mary's* as she comes out of the Patuxent estuary into the Chesapeake.

According to a despatch from Commander Wells, the vessel selected and seized by Brain was a fast schooner of 115 tons, built in Baltimore and registered at St. Mary's, Maryland. She carried passengers and 'an assorted cargo valued at $20,000'.

Official U.S. naval records show that there was another *St. Mary's* in existence. She had been scuttled in the St. John's River alongside the yacht *America* which had been sailed across the Atlantic to win the Royal Yacht Squadron's (America) Cup in 1851, to the surprise of certain British yachtsmen of the day. Both ships had been scuttled to save them from Confederate forces when they occupied Jacksonville for a few months in the winter of 1861–62. By 12 March the city was recaptured and Lieutenant (afterwards Rear Admiral) Stevens was sent by Admiral Du Pont to raise the oddly assorted pair. He describes this *St. Mary's* as 'a fine and valuable steamer'. They were both later armed for anti-privateer and blockade work.

One has become so used, by now, to Brain's seizure of steamships that before examining sources which have come to light through the good offices of the editor of *The Gleaner* (Jamaica), and the U.S. naval records, one might have supposed that it was this steamship that Brain was interested in. But a moment's thought is enough to convince anyone that a fully-rigged, seaworthy sailing vessel was the most efficient and, indeed, only practical answer under the then prevailing circumstances. Not only had he had learned his lesson, in both the *Roanoke* and the

Ocean-going schooner of similar type to the *St. Mary's*

Chesapeake, as to the Achilles heel of these early steamers, with their rapacious and inefficient furnaces which restricted operations to short passages, but from then on there would be no coaling stations available to him. The last two Confederate ports of Wilmington and Charleston had fallen to the enemy forces two months previously and even neutral ports were closing their doors because of the imminent defeat of the Southern States.

Hence, I am convinced this was his reasoning when he chose to attack and capture an armed schooner and not another steamship for his privateering operations over the next few months. And so the *St. Mary's* became the last warship ever to wear the flag of the Confederate States Navy on the Atlantic seaboard.

The date, 1 April, is also significant as being the day before General Lee was finally driven from his battered capital of Richmond and eight days before he sat down in the quiet little court house of Appomatox with General Grant to arrange terms of surrender for the Confederate armies and so terminate one of the most sanguinary and ferocious wars of modern history. At midday on 2 April Rear Admiral Semmes, commanding the James River squadron, was at dinner in the *Virginia* when he got his last instructions from the Confederate Navy Department.

> Sir. General Lee advises the Government to withdraw from this city, the Officers will leave this evening. . . . upon you is devolved the duty of destroying your ships this night, and with all the forces under your command joining Gen. Lee.
>
> S. R. Mallory, Secretary of the Navy

That night the ironclads of the last Confederate squadron were blown up and the wooden gunboats set alight and allowed to drift downstream. Apart from the *Shenandoah* (Captain Waddell) somewhere in the Pacific, the *St. Mary's* was now the only Confederate ship still afloat and actively carrying on the war at sea.

Brain wasted no time and by dawn next day he had managed to sail the *St. Mary's* clean through the flotilla of blockading cruisers, round Cape Charles opposite the Norfolk Naval Base and clear away into the open Atlantic. The trickiest bit through the narrows, only fifteen miles wide, was of course accomplished under cover of darkness and we happen to know that during the previous hours of daylight he was helped by the fact that there was a full gale blowing from the north-east. This knowledge comes from the log of a brother officer, Captain Fitzhugh, who had also made an attempt to capture the S.S. *Louisiana* the same night, but failed to board her because, as he later stated, 'a heavy gale was blowing and the seas were running high'.

Having got safely out of the dangerous narrow waters of the Chesapeake, Brain must have calculated that the U.S. navy would assume he would be making south for the West Indies, as the best and most obvious sphere of operations for a Confederate privateer cruiser. So, he turns north where he will be least expected, and before midday on the same morning (2 April) has closed with and captured another prize, a large, sea-going schooner, the *J. B. Spafford*, on passage from Wicomico to New York. She had a full cargo of wood, which was of no interest to the Confederates, but, instead of destroying her, Brain transferred to her the captain, passengers and crew of the *St. Mary's*, except two crew members who were sworn into the Confederate Navy and retained to help work the ship. Then the *Spafford* was released to continue her voyage to New York, her master having been told by Brain that he was 'going to St. Mark's, Florida'. I imagine this was a rather transparent plant, in the hopes it would put the naval authorities off the scent.

This action had taken place off Hog Island, Northampton County on the Maryland coast and was concluded in no small hurry because the *St. Mary's* skipper had already spotted another useful victim on passage up the coast. The second capture was made in the late afternoon and the ship burned—after the crew and anything of value had been salvaged, presumably. Then he turned back towards the West Indies, because when the master of the *Spafford* reached Lewes he reported to the U.S. naval commander, from whose despatch I quote,

The *St. Mary's* was last seen by the released crew, heading to the south, with the wind from the northward and they report that there was a light in a south easterly direction which they supposed was a vessel the rebels had captured and set fire to.

If the wind held, Brain would take a bit of catching as the *St. Mary's* would be capable of a good fifteen knots, unencumbered by furnaces or propeller drag. And by the time it dropped he would be well out into the Atlantic and would have the element of surprise each time he re-entered the shipping lanes in search of prey. It was an encouraging start. In two days, while dodging a number of enemy cruisers busy searching for him, he had captured three sea-going vessels and disposed of his initial prize, the yawl.

In passing, I think it would be worth noting, for those unfamiliar with sailing ships, that the size of the vessel chosen to become the privateer herself would have been very much conditioned by the size of Commander Brain's Confederate crew, numbering ten only. As we have seen, he had been able to add the two Union men, from the *St. Mary's* original crew, who had been persuaded to sign on with the Confederates. Now, except for the dog watches, the standard watches would be 4 hours on and 8 hours off every 12 hours. This would be a heavy drain on the energy of 12 crew members out of which would have to come a cook, carpenter, sailmaker and mate or boatswain in between whiles. Any change of sail, such as shortening for the night or for increase of wind, or even going about, would call for the services of all watches whatever time of the day or night it might be. In addition there were cruisers to dodge, commercial ships to capture and search and the forward and aft swivel guns to be manned and maintained. There cannot have been much time to sit about and bite nails.

It meant there were no spare hands for prize crews on captured vessels, but fortunately that problem would not arise because there was nowhere to send captured ships anyway; they could only be put up for sale in neutral ports! Until there was definite news of the cessation of hostilities it would be necessary to capture vessels fairly regularly in order to renew stocks of food and, more important, water. Except for relatively small and valuable cargoes which could be transferred easily and sold in neutral ports for ammunition, or better, long-range, rifled guns, the vessels and cargoes would have to be burned, as most of Brain's fellow privateers on both sides had done before. The crew and any passengers were generally allowed to go ashore in the ship's boats if the weather was reasonable. If this were not possible, they were merely dumped aboard the next capture which would be allowed to proceed under bond after the extraction of anything useful.

However, from time to time, there would be a need for harbour facilities, not only for repairs but simply to give the crew a break ashore in some remote spot where, perhaps, the authorities were known to be a bit lax—as in the Spanish Islands. Or so one might have supposed with any more cautious and normal skipper.

But, as we know by now, Brain isn't a normal commander and, true to form, while the West Indies squadron was happily combing the remote islands, he calmly sails into the main British port of Nassau—where he is least expected—as bold as brass, flying the Confederate flag at the peak. We hear of this from the United States Consul, Thomas Kirkpatrick. Brain's official reason for the visit was for repairs that could only be effected with modern harbour facilities, but the despatch also hints at another reason which Brain would have kept very quiet about—better armament for the *St. Mary's*. Like other armed schooners of her size she could carry only two guns conveniently and safely without a lot of strengthening of decks, a bow gun and a stern chaser. As her original armament would have been fairly low down on the Union priority for the smaller sea-going vessels, her guns were probably old smooth bores which were inaccurate except at short range and had in any case a relatively short carry.

Brain would have been after some of the new rifled guns which had, by then, been installed in most naval ships. They had twice the range and were immeasurably more accurate. He would need matching ammunition also, and probably Nassau or Bermuda would be the only establishments where such things were available—at a price. To pay for this and for provisions, he had valuable cargo to sell.

There is another intriguing little question at this juncture. I have no means of knowing whether our commander and his Confederate crew had just not heard from any captured vessel that the war was virtually over when General Lee, the Confederate Commander-in-Chief, capitulated at Appomatox on 9 April, or whether they had decided, like a number of other scattered units, to carry on a war of their own. It is true that General Johnson's army of the South did not surrender to Sherman until 26 April and General Kirby Smith held out round Shrevefort until 28 May in distant Louisiana. I know that news travelled slowly where the telegraph could not reach in those pre-wireless days but, if Brain did know, he must have taken a hair-raising risk that he would be able to get his guns and provisions aboard and clear from Nassau before the news became generally known. His luck held and he was officially treated with full belligerent rights—to the intense fury of the American Consul, who brought all the pressure he could muster upon the British authorities to seize the ship and imprison the crew. Let me quote from his despatch:

Letter from the U.S. Consul at Nassau, New Providence to Acting Rear-Admiral Stribling U.S. Navy regarding the seizure of the American Schooner St. Mary's by party commanded by John Brain.

U.S. Consulate
Nassau, April 22nd, 1865

Dear Sir,

Since I wrote you a few days ago there has arrived in this port the American Schooner St. Mary's of Baltimore with full cargo captured from her Master . . . in Chesapeake Bay about 1 o'clock on the morning of April 1st, 1865. [Then follows a note of her subsequent doings as already set out.] I immediately applied to the Government here to have the vessel seized, with her piratical crew. They declined, saying she was a legitimate prize, and she put to sea again having put in here under the plea of distress. She is commanded and was seized by the notorious John C. Brain of steamers Chesapeake and Roanoke notoriety . . . The name of the schooner has been erased.

Yours in haste

Thomas Kirkpatrick

Admiral C. K. Stribling

I have omitted some rather hysterical pleading that Admiral Stribling with his East Gulf blockading squadron should do all in his power 'to procure this man's capture and end his career of guilt'. Also, having tried to bring charges of piracy and been told firmly by the British Government authorities that the charges were nonsense and the *St. Mary's* was a perfectly legitimate Confederate prize, he even fell back on the old trumped-up piracy charge that had been tried and failed in the Canadian courts at the time of the capture of the *Chesapeake*. This had no better result and Brain was given a clean bill of health as a perfectly legitimate commerce raider. This was indeed quite correct because, though the Commander-in-Chief had surrendered the forces under his immediate command, President Jefferson Davies and his cabinet had urged continuation of hostilities, that is, until they themselves were rounded up and captured on 10 May.

The *Bahama Herald* of 19 April was also full of it.

Arrival: The Confederate States Prize Schooner 'St. Mary's' (Lieut. John C. Brain Commander) arrived at Salt Cays on Monday . . . On Captain Brain's producing his commission and orders, His Excellency Gov. Rawson immediately gave orders for her release and kindly granted her permission to remain for the space of twenty-four hours to obtain the necessary supplies of water and wood.

There is more, not very relevant, information, and then the delightful assertion that 'Captain Brain had no sextant or chart aboard'. The theory is then expounded that he had followed Drake's precedent and obtained his position from ships he boarded or hailed. But he does not seem to have been very successful, because by the time he entered Nassau Harbour the ship's crew were down to a pint of water per man per day.

The U.S. Consul, Kirkpatrick, did however let drop one bit of information about Brain's next move and the probable location of his next operations against Union shipping. Either the Consul's intelligence service was very good or some of the Confederate sailors had been opening their mouths a little wider than was wise in the local taverns—or probably both. Kirkpatrick was able to tell the Admiral that 'It is supposed here that he [Brain] has gone to Spanish Wells or Harbour Islands to get H. A. Paw'. Obviously this was his old comrade in arms Lieutenant H. A. Parr who had been with him in all his raids on enemy shipping.

10

Harbour Islands, by the way, are a few miles up the North-West Providence Channel which was the short way back to the Gulf Stream, the Florida coast and one of the densest shipping lanes in the world. One has to admire Brain's nerve! I have no written evidence as to what Parr had been doing but I think it was pretty obvious that while Brain was busy publicly with his repairs, Parr (probably under an assumed name) had been secretly buying and transporting to Harbour Islands the ammunition and the new replacement guns, which would have been confiscated if put aboard openly in Nassau.

Anyway, the *St. Mary's* was not intercepted by any cruisers of Admiral Stribling as she left the vicinity of Harbour Islands but the hunt was now localised and the whole resources of the U.S. Florida and West Indian squadrons were free to concentrate upon the last Confederate raider afloat in the area.

We soon get news that, amongst others, the British gunboat *Fawn* was hot on the trail. We hear this from the Resident of the Turks and Caicos Islands who sent a despatch to the Governor of Jamaica on 17 May.

> Sir, My attention having been called to a paragraph in the *Bahama Herald* of the 19th of April last, which I annex, and having heard a rumour of one of Her Majesty's ships being in chase of a suspicious schooner, I requested the Receiver General to assertain from the master of a Nassau vessel which had just arrived, what information he was in possession of on the subject and I now do myself the honour to transmit to your excellency the statement made to that officer by Capt. Joseph Phillips, the master of this schooner *Charles Turmell* of Nassau. . .

There is more of that splendid sentence, which for sheer official gobbledygook is unbeatable; but I turn to the skipper's statement.

> On Tuesday the 2nd of May, off Cat Island, I met with the Steam Ship *Fawn* and was enquired of if I had seen any schooner passing through the passage, as the Commander was in search of the Confederate Prize Schooner . . . called the *Mary* which had

recently left Nassau under suspicious circumstances, and he
advised me to be on my guard if I met with her. I reached
Sapadilla Bay on the south side of the Blue Hill, Caicos on
Tuesday the 9th of May . . . I here found . . . Schooner answer-
ing the description given me by the Commander of the *Fawn*.
The next day the Commander of the Schooner referred to came
on board.

Then follows an enchanting account of how Brain in his turn
cross-questions Phillips very thoroughly as to the positions of the
British and American warships that he has met on passage or that
were in Nassau when he left the port—good cat and mouse stuff.
Brain invites him back aboard, naturally enough, for a drink and
Phillips records having seen ten members of crew—but no armaments (which I imagine by that time had all been safely stowed
away below) except one 'double barrelled fowling piece'. This was
displayed as a joke, we gather, in typical J.C.B. fashion. And it did
not fool skipper Phillips, because he continues his report, 'I was,
however, informed by some of the crew of the other vessels lying
there that they had been busy cleaning arms and running balls on
board the said Schooner . . .'.
Like others, he noticed that the name had been erased and on
asking what it was, was told the 'S.S.'. Indeed, this appears on
several other reports of sightings in the area. There is only one
doubt, in that he quotes the ship as being about half the known
size, but I imagine it was the *St. Mary's* all right, because the ten
men and everything else fits. They must have encountered some
heavy weather, because they were reported as having had some
assistance in repairing their sails.
The *Charles Turmell* left on 11 May, leaving the *St. Mary's* riding
at anchor, but it was understood that she would be leaving next
day; which indeed she did, on the tide. And from that day until
9 June the *St. Mary's* simply disappears into the blue. The hunt is
still very much on, by both navies and with pilots that knew the
channels and reefs and deep water anchorages like the back of
their hand. Brain must have had, in addition to his penchant for
survival, a reasonable modicum of navigational skill to cope with
some of the trickiest waterways in the world for a month without,

we gather, quite as many charts as the modern yachtsman takes nowadays.

Most significantly there was an uncanny silence, not only on the part of the newspapers like the *Bahama Herald* and *Jamaica Daily Gleaner and Star*, which had no news to give the public, but also a search of the respective archives has produced no naval or official Government despatches with a reference. There is, to my mind, only one logical explanation. Brain had at last got the message that the official war really was not only over but lost and it was high time that the guns were put away for good and the *St. Mary's* and her crew returned to normal peacetime pursuits. In any case he knew she would have to be handed over in due course to the British authorities for return to the conquering North. It was imperative to stop chasing American coastal shipping and he must have done this otherwise the newspapers would have made a meal of it, because then it would have been actual and unjustifiable piracy, in the eyes of the world as well as the biassed Northern papers. The Confederates probably either ditched their guns or, more likely, sold them profitably on some remote island.

And the time lag of a month? This, I suggest, has an even more delightfully simple answer. The crew at this point reckoned they had done a reasonably good job and deserved a holiday before they returned to a starving battle-torn country or emigrated. So, as there did not seem to be any point in falling over themselves to return their dream ship to an ungrateful regime, they filled in the pleasant month of May with a sort of relaxing 'adventure holiday' cruise through the islands—before the weather got uncomfortably hot! The chase by British and American warships must have added a sort of spice to what might otherwise have become a bit humdrum. They evaded capture however and on Friday, 9 June, calmly arrived off Kingston, the capital city of Jamaica, and dropped anchor.

The *Aboukir*, the flagship of the West Indies squadron, wearing the flag of Commodore Cracroft, was in port and there was more than a slight stir. I will let Cracroft's despatch to Governor Eyre speak for itself.

Aboukir at Jamaica. . . . The Confederate States Prize Schooner

St. Mary's arrived off this port on Friday (9th June) night last and anchored outside . . . I sent a boat . . . the officer in charge acquainted my Secretary that Captain Brain and Lieutenant Edenborough were away at Kingston.

Quite rightly, they had gone ashore in the ship's boat to make arrangements for handing over the *St. Mary's*, if required to do so as expected, or even, as a later despatch suggests, prepared to draw provisions if it looked as though they would be allowed to proceed as a peaceful merchant ship. It is curious that, as it seems from all the official reports, they were still being accorded full rights and courtesies as belonging to a Confederation of States that no longer existed and this was obviously what set up a renewed howl of rage from both the naval and consular authorities of the United States.

The Confederate lieutenant left in charge of the *St. Mary's* by Brain had quite correctly told the Commodore's secretary that the orders from the captain had been 'not to come into port because three months had not elapsed since they were in a British Colonial Port and therefore he thought he could not legally enter'. He went on to add that 'the desire and intention of them all was to get to England and they didn't care what became of the schooner'.

The next day, 13 June, the Governor astonished everybody by replying to Commodore Cracroft that 'Permission was granted for the *St. Mary's* to enter the Port of Kingston to obtain supplies'. The American authorities were both astonished and unhappy at this decision. It meant that the *St. Mary's* was temporarily safe from capture on the high seas and possession would entail a long, probably heated, legal wrangle in the courts instead. This left Governor Eyre quite unmoved and next day, on the 14th, he sat down and wrote to the Secretary of State for the Colonies, enclosing a despatch (50/6744) from the Turks Island Resident about the *St. Mary's* and passing on the results of Commodore Cracroft's inspection of the ship, already referred to above. He added, 'The Captain, Lieutenants and eight crew . . . appeared to be civilly and peaceably inclined, having in their possession no arms save three old muskets . . . their desire was merely to enter the Port of Kingston to obtain supplies of which they were greatly in need'.

Another despatch states that there were armaments and other stores hidden away which were sold or sent to England, presumably to pay for repatriation of those members of the crew who, like Brain, did not go to England but preferred to return to the Southern States (which is where we next hear of him).

Perhaps I should say, in passing, that the poor old *St. Mary's* herself was by no means finished and she continued to keep the government offices of two nations busy for some time. While the British Government back home was considering the despatch from Governor Eyre there was all hell let loose in Kingston itself. The United States authorities were claiming the restitution of the vessel; the local British authorities had put her up for sale and the original owners had been notified and were putting in their claim. Counsel's opinion was being sought left, right and centre—in fact the legal boys were having an off-season bonanza. Even the U.S. Secretary of State, William Seward, was engaged in heated correspondence with Earl Russell, the British Foreign Secretary, about her return to her American owner. And then, suddenly, an almost incomprehensible despatch arrived from H.M. Government in England, possibly aimed at cutting the Gordian knot.

Mr. Hugh Austin, Government Secretarial Office, Kingston, wrote via the Principal Officer of Customs, Kingston, to

The Commander or Person in charge of the Schooner *St. Mary* on the 5th July 65.

Sir, I am commanded by His Excellency the Governor of Jamaica, to direct you in accordance with instructions given His Excellency by HMG to leave the Jamaica Waters in twenty four hours after you receive this notice,

I have etc.

The next day the Principal Officer of Customs 'has the honour' to reply that the instructions have been complied with. He adds at the end that rumours have arrived that she has been set on fire and abandoned between Pedro Cays and the Cayman Islands—that was 7 July. It may be that this was Brain's last act of frustration at the interminable delays in disposing of the *St. Mary's* legally after he had complied with international law by surrendering her to the local British authorities. It was known that he wished to return to Georgia, taking advantage of President Johnson's amnesty of 29 May for all Confederate personnel who were prepared to take the oath of allegiance to the Union. It may even have been the combination of irritation at being suddenly and inexplicably told by the British authorities to take her to sea again and an understandable determination that in that event at least his last command was not going to fall intact into the hands of a grasping Union Government. I don't know. There is no mention of Brain in the local reports. Only, to cut a very long story short, the *St. Mary's* was sighted, on fire, by Captain Eden of the British armed brigantine *Ruatan*. He was able to extinguish the fire with the help of Lieutenant Edenborough and four ex-Confederate crew who were rowing to the shore but returned. It is even possible that Edenborough had been the only member of the original crew aboard the *St. Mary's* in Kingston harbour when the order came through and had been told by the Principal Customs Officer to 'beat it' somewhere, anywhere, so long as the customs could say the *St. Mary's* had departed as ordered. Edenborough, not having a notion what to do with the vessel, put a match to her; and Captain Eden of the *Ruatan* (according to despatch No. 203 from the Governor to the Secretary of State, kindly supplied by the Jamaican Archives, Spanish Town) then towed the wreck into the Cayman Islands where the Justices allowed him 75% of the salvage. This was promptly quashed by the Attorney General, Kingston, at the instigation of the American Vice-Consul.

So ended the last voyage of the *St. Mary's* out of Baltimore. Whatever you may feel about it—especially the slightly saucy post-war cruise extension—the old schooner is on record as the last vessel on active service on the Atlantic seaboard to fly the battle ensign of the Confederate States of America at her masthead.

'No Evidence to Criminate Him'

THE CIRCUS WAS A ROARING SUCCESS—AS A PRELUDE TO PRISON

Though the end of the *St. Mary's* marked also the end of John Clibbon Brain's sea-going activities, it was not yet the end of the ex-commander and his faithful crew members. His penchant for survival still held good and by October of the same year, 1865, after a quick visit to Liverpool and the Bannut Tree House to see his Uncle Frederick, he was back in Georgia among the few wartime friends who had been lucky enough to survive the ravages of four terrible years.

He and his men returned to a devastation that is almost impossible to describe—to a South starved into surrender and pounded into peace; a country where the post-war ravages by Union troops and civilian 'carpet baggers' were far more thorough than the military damage of four years of war. 260,000 men had been killed in the vastly smaller (numerically speaking) South, and the maimed and missing were never even counted. This represented approximately one-fifth of the productive male population. The remainder, as a reporter in Georgia noted, were 'aimless young men in grey, ragged and filthy who seemed to have lost their object in life'. Most of them, as the historian Dixon Wecter wrote, 'had had to ask for handouts on the road home, with nothing to exchange for bread save the unwelcome news of Appomatox'. For those at home it was a case of 'Furl that Banner, softly, slowly! . . . For its people's hopes are dead.' Indeed, the weakening of purpose, morale and 'will to recover' among the survivors was, in the words of another historian, William Miller, 'depressing enough to make many of these survivors envy the dead'.

As you may have gathered by now, Brain was never one to sit down and feel sorry for himself and he seems also to have felt a sort of moral responsibility for the welfare of his wartime crew. As he sat down with them, in what was left of some up country tavern, to tot up his assets, he must have realised that he had few professional qualifications to build on—other than a certain facility for capturing enemy ships, leading men into action and women into the more delightful realms of l'amour, wine and song. Sensibly enough, he simply cashes in on what he can of these attributes, however inadequate they might appear not only in peacetime but in a countryside beaten to its knees and smarting under an unsympathetic army of occupation.

With his comrades' enthusiastic co-operation he devises and runs a circus, to relieve the general gloom in the villages and provide at least a modicum of daily bread and butter. I gather from letters and news that filtered back home that it was a roaring success—for a time. Rather like the mystery and morality plays that used to tour the English countryside in medieval times, they re-enacted scenes from their wartime adventures, freely interspersed with distinctly original sea shanties, doubtful sailors' songs, and ballads which had more enthusiasm and panache than either tact or literary merit. In fact it was mostly good 'cowboys and Indians' stuff—except, of course, that the United States forces, the Northerners, had taken the place of the Indians in this early *ad hoc* forerunner of our modern 'Westerns' and each episode invariably resounded to the immortal memory of the Confederates, who were the 'goodies'.

The dispirited people of the little country towns and villages loved it and the passage of the circus from place to place became almost a royal progress. Quite obviously this could not last for ever and eventually the occupying authorities caught up with them and the circus was firmly closed and the 'performers' were lucky to escape, once more, to the woods and oblivion. As soon as the ballyhoo had subsided and the heat was off, mostly because the Union forces had more serious matters, such as looting, and the reconstruction of railways and profitable factories, to deal with, we find John Clibbon Brain re-emerging in the more sober and respectable occupation of artist.

In fact he really did settle down for the first time in his young life in the country where, by now, his affections lay. He bought a house in the heart of war-torn Confederate country, at Savannah, Georgia, a district which had escaped the worst excesses of the Union troops. It was not far from the two erstwhile Southern blockade running ports of Charleston and Wilmington and had the added attraction that a number of wartime friends also had their homes there or along the adjacent South Carolina coast.

We find him practising as an artist and, like his father, as an engraver and illustrator of books and pamphlets. In spite of the disrupted state of commerce and the general lack of money owing to the change of currency he not only managed to make both ends meet but had enough over to make a home both for his two young daughters and for his mother, who came south to live with him. Brain's father was by now dead, so she was a widow. But it must be said that though he, with his affectionate nature and soft spot for his father (as his letters show), would have missed him, I doubt whether his mother would have noticed any change in her financial situation. Anyway she was only too pleased to be reunited with her son. There is no news of his wife after their wartime home at Holly Springs, Missouri, was broken up. There they had had two daughters during the infrequent visits between chasing ships and now he was once more able to provide a home for them and see to their education. Georgia, especially in the spring when the mimosa trees are out and the scented shrubs fill the still evenings with their sharp sweetness, is a pleasant country and the reunited family enjoyed it to the full.

By summer the engraving was going well and people in the little county town were only too glad to enjoy the opportunity of being able to buy a few artistic bits and pieces to brighten up the dull routine of living. John Clibbon Brain would have fitted readily and cosily into any society, with his pleasant manner and ability to talk freely to all manner of men—and he had no shortage of things to talk about. One might be forgiven for thinking, as I am sure Brain himself did, that his troubles were over. The amnesty promulgated by President Andrew Johnson as long ago as 29 May the previous year seemed to be working well and Brain had duly taken the oath of allegiance to the United States.

But it was not to be. On 13 September of that year (1866),

exactly one year and five months after the guns had fallen silent, there was a knock at the door of the Wall House in Williamsburg (Va.) where Brain was staying with friends. It was an odd knock, not neighbourly but loud with the note of authority in it, and military boots sounded on the cobbles.

Brain was yet again under arrest and, rather unnecessarily I think, put in irons and taken to the 45th Precinct Station House where, as he said, 'I was kept all night without bedding of any kind. I took cold that night'.

He was examined yet again by U.S. Commissioner Newton, and all the old claptrap of Confederate privateers being classed as pirates and murderers under the United States naval code was raked up once more, in spite of the amnesty and in spite of the Bill of Rights. In spite, even, of the 14th amendment which had just been passed by Congress, Brain was whisked off to the Brooklyn Penitentiary where he was kept, as it ultimately turned out, for three years without trial or even any specific charges being preferred.

The reign of terror of the Doges of Venice had nothing on the democratic fervour of the United States Congress smelling out Confederate privateers now that they were disarmed and safe to handle. As Mark Twain remarked when a Venetian committee of public safety received anonymous accusations against loyal citizens, 'If the committee could find no proof to support an accusation it usually found the accused guilty anyhow, on the ground that the lack of proof simply showed how deep and devious the man's villiany really was'.

Public conscience had degenerated to such a state that it was now almost a crime to invoke the Bill of Rights. The Union had been saved—but at a price. The price was that American traditional freedom had temporarily lapsed: I mean, the freedom that the originators of the tradition meant should apply equally to those we disagree with, as well as to the 'yes men' of the political bandwaggons. The real test of course always comes when people have been badly frightened and civil war is a frightening experience for a nation to go through. The 14th amendment of 13 June 1866, incorporating the Civil Rights Act into the Constitution specifically stated 'Nor shall any state deprive any person of life, liberty or property, without due process of law'. Ironically enough, this had been promulgated just three months before Brain was again thrown into prison and kept there for three years without any official charge being preferred and without any pretence of a trial. I can only think that this operation was the last move of the extremists in the United States Congress and even they were forced in the end to admit that it was a travesty of justice.

The Union itself had used privateers freely in the wars with Great Britain and all the major nations had recognised during the Civil War 'The armed ships of both belligerents, whether public ships of war or privateers'.

This meant, of course, official privateers sailing under Letters of Marque for which there were very strict rules laid down by both governments, according to the generally accepted international law prevailing at that time. Both Brain and other privateer captains such as Waddell of the *Shenandoah*, who was similarly charged by Secretary Welles, held not only commissions in the Confederate Navy but had Letters of Marque duly signed by the President himself in the presence of two witnesses. Waddell, who finished up in a British port was immediately cleared and set free by the 'Officers of the Crown' who told the Union representatives under Mr. Adams quite firmly that they were talking moonshine. In addition they pointed out that the United States Congress itself had, in March 1863 passed a bill authorising the President to issue Letters of Marque, in order, as the *New York Herald* said grandiloquently, 'to cause the ocean to swarm with our militia of the seas'.

Unfortunately for Brain, he was on United States soil and it took the naval authorities, who were understandably needled by the exploits of an amateur sailor, three years to come to the confeclusion that they could not have it both ways and any sort of trial would make them the laughing stock of the world. In fairness we must add that, in addition to the real damage done by the Conderate privateers during the war, neither Brain's popularity among the common people of the South nor his post-war activities in the 'Circus' would have endeared him to the establishment.

As Scharf points out in his *History*,[17]

They [official privateers] scrupulously refrained from interference with the personal property of individuals . . . and every passenger was set on shore without harm or loss. 'Pirates' would have cleaned out their pockets as thoroughly as Sherman swept the homes of Georgia, or Sheridan those of the Shenandoah Valley.

The latter was, indeed, only too true, but naturally it excited no comment in a completely partisan Northern press, who were much too busy berating all Confederate initiative on the high seas. A Southern privateer was a pirate; a Northern privateer was a hero—it was as simple as that.

At first Brain tried enlisting the help of the more responsible papers in an effort at least to be brought to trial or to learn on what specific charges he was being held; but all to no avail. In fairness to the press, however, I must say it was their campaigning and re-awakening of the public conscience that at the end of three long years forced the legal authorities to admit that as they could find no charges that would hold any water in a court, Brain must be released unconditionally even though still with no apology or amends.

To show you the not very edifying sort of journalism (by present standards) that had to be sprayed on to the general public before officials could be moved to action, I quote part of an interview which covered a long column on the main page of the powerful *New York Daily Tribune* for Saturday, 20 February 1869.

THE LAST OF THE CONFEDERATES

A Man Without a Country—The Case of Lieutenant Brain— his offence and the story of his imprisonment.

When that vivid fiction, 'The Man Without a Country' was first published, the American people were startled at the bare possibility of its truthfulness, and the very extravagance of the conception contributed to its plausibility. Philip Nolan has almost a parallel in John C. Brain. Arrested in 1866 upon a charge of piracy and murder, he is still in Brooklyn Penitentiary in 1869 untried and unconvicted. Seeing but few visitors and constantly surrounded by convicts he is held in confinement without trial when Andrew Johnson's pardons have reached everybody beside and opened the prison doors to worse than he. Brain has repeatedly been 'written up' in the newspapers during the years of his confinement; at one time he was represented as in Brooklyn jail, an arrogant and bitter rebel breathing worn out maledictions against the government, with a face like that of the Richmond hack-driver, who said the other day 'Confederate money will be good yet. Kribby Smith is still fighten' across the Mississippi and he will bring it up'. At another time the story is that he is languishing in the penitentiary broken in health and shattered in intellect an object of pity rather than a subject of punishment; and then the months turn their weary round and he is forgotten but still a prisoner. The indictment so long impending over Jefferson Davis, no longer hangs suspended like the uplifted blade of a guillotine ready to fall on the neck of a proud and wilful traitor conquered but not subdued; Brecknidge, who left the Senate of the United States in their time of war to engage in the struggle against the government which had cherished him, is free to return to the country he betrayed; Semmes, the modern corsair, than whom even Byron's Giaour is no worse, may clap the loudest approval of the Clarendon–Johnson treaty for the settlement of the Alabama claims; but one poor wretch, not so bad as these, is left to suffer because he was not so prominent.

The next paragraph or two merely deal with the experiences of various people who called at the jail and found the prison filled with convicts and described the 'villainous smoke and sombre looks that were in strange contrast to the fresh air and cheerful skies without'. Then follows an interview by one of the reporters 'who had first seen Brain at the time of his examination before the U.S. Commissioner Newton in September'.

He then had an opportunity to ask for Lieutenant Brain. After a brief delay, the consent of Brain to the visit having been first obtained, he was taken for the interview into the well-warmed and lighted corridor. The prisoner cheerfully reached out one hand by way of friendly welcome while in the other he held his pipe and tobacco pouch, the solace of his prison hours. The formalities of the interview being over, pencil and paper were soon at work tracing the story which had been told in the newspapers before but this time it came from Brain's own lips, and in his own way. Long after the heat and passion of the war had passed, and with his proud spirit mellowed, if not overcome by confinement and suffering, it has a new interest and a personal charm. He said: My name is John C. Brain—not Braine—and I was a First Lieutenant in the Confederate Navy.

This of course was perfectly correct, because his rank of commander was only acting for the period of the war; and perhaps I should explain that for some reason his name had appeared throughout the war with an 'e' at the end.

I will not give the main part of the interview because it simply covers a certain number of the incidents which have been written up in this book and would thus essentially be boring. But one very interesting fact does emerge. Brain explained that his commission and various orders were lost during or after the war, and reminded the interviewer that the archives of the Confederate Naval Department had been destroyed by the Federal forces and so it was impossible to obtain original papers deposited there. And then he went on to say something which I think is important and convincing:

But I have placed affidavits in the hands of the Attorney General of the United States setting out all the facts of the case. These affidavits are by Stephen R. Mallory, the Secretary of the Confederate Navy, Dr. Jones, Auditor, and Mr. Tidball, Chief Clerk to the Navy Department, Admiral Semmes, Captain Mafitt and others.

This I think finally disposes of any doubt there may have been as to the authenticity and genuineness of the commission and written instructions for the capture of the steamship (name to be filled in when the choice had been made on the spot) and Letters of Marque duly signed by the President before witnesses. For obvious reasons the name *Chesapeake* had to be filled in later.

None of the papers for the other captures have, to my knowledge, ever been questioned. But the publication of written affidavits signed by people of the standing of the Secretary of State for the Navy and the naval Commander in Chief at the end of the war, Admiral Semmes, convinces one beyond all doubt that the attempts by the United States authorities to cast doubt on some of the papers were purely vindictive and complete moonshine because, of course, the *New York Daily Tribune* had every chance in the world to check up on these affidavits with the signatories and would have done so for its own sake before printing the paragraph.

I don't think we get any new information from the description of the various actions and their recapitulation by the *Tribune*, as full accounts have already been incorporated in the book. Poor Brain invited the reporter to make it clear to the general public that he was hardly 'the bloodthirsty individual' that he has been represented to be. In fact the article goes on to say,

Lieutenant Brain was a tall, straight and commanding looking personage when in health but his sufferings in prison have been so intense that he cannot walk without the aid of a crutch and is, perhaps, permanently disabled. His right foot is much swollen from inflammatory rheumatism, a disease he attributes to the unavoiadble dampness of the prison and he is indeed a wreck of the man who entered it nearly three years ago. He is only 29 years of age but says, with truthfulness that is apparent in his looks, that since his imprisonment he has grown old faster than the flight of years. He is a man of mild and affable manners and agreeable conversation and seems in his bearing to have kept himself untainted from the prison atmosphere about him. A widowed mother and two young daughters depend on him for support and he expresses himself as anxious to be with them. Efforts are being made to secure his pardon at the hands of President Johnson, but if he is not pardoned, the Constitution guarantees him a speedy trial, and it is made the duty of the courts and the Government to see that this is not only accorded to him but insisted upon. Had either of these things been done that wretched spectacle of a man, not convicted of any crime, compelled to be the daily companion of convicted felons would not now offend the nobler instincts of the American people. . . . That was a sad and painful record which the hand of the story writer traced in the life of Philip Nolan but here is a man without a country and without a trial whose few years of suffering reverse the natural order, and make the truth of his story look for a parallel in the tales of fiction.

The lameness was to remain with him for life, as we hear of it again thirty years later from the *Confederate Veteran*.

Well, that appeared in February 1869. I have omitted some of the contemporary journalese as it is apt to jar on the modern reader, but it must be remembered that even 100 years ago American reporters had to 'make it good' or nobody would listen to them. By that time, the imprisonment of a man who became known as the 'Last of the Confederate Privateers' had become almost a cause célèbre. Papers like the *Courier-Journal* of Louisville, Kentucky, which carried long paragraphs on Captain Brain on 23 February, 26th, and on 6 March 1869, all supported the *New York Daily Tribune* in its campaign.

The clamour for his release mounted; petitions to the authorities were circulated and signed by a wide range of people of normally dissimilar interests and the President himself was bombarded by requests from deputations of both public and private citizens. I quote two typical extracts from the *Louisville Courier—Journal*:

Colonel Blanton-Duncan is circulating a petition for the release of Captain J. C. Braine, the only remaining Confederate prisoner of war, and it will, in a day or so be presented to the President. This release is asked for without reference to the legal aspects of the case. It is already signed by a number of influential Radicals and more Democrats.

Three days later the 'Ladies of Baltimore' go into action—and even the President quails:

A deputation of Baltimore Ladies, Mrs. John Hanson-Thomas,

11

Mrs. Getting, and others, accompanied by Senator Whyte, waited on the President to-day to urge the pardon of Capt. Braine. Mrs. Getting said, 'In a few days, Mr. President, you will receive the hospitality of Baltimore and her heartfelt welcome. Amid the joys of that occasion do not permit even a thought to mar the harmony, or allow it to be said the cry of anguish still ascends, unheeded from the prisoner in his cell, the solitary memento of that ruthless war for which we are not responsible.' The President's reply was of a cheering character and indicated that this appeal, together with the strongly intentioned petition submitted to him will assure the release of the unfortunate man. Attorney-General Evarts has been instructed to make a report on the case to the President.

Who wouldn't quail a bit?

By late spring Brain was again a free man, almost, one might say, by this time basking in the uncertain sunshine of public sympathy and in great demand as a speaker at town meetings and rehabilitation and fund raising societies. But first he went north to stay with his sister, Lucy Hamilton, and her family at Longueuil just outside Montreal. His mother, who naturally enough went there when he was imprisoned, also welcomed him, and there was a very happy family reunion. I have a contemporary cutting from the *Montreal Commercial Advertiser*, sent to my grandfather by Lucy Hamilton, which also published 'Documents relating to the imprisonment . . . of Mr. John C. Brain, an artist who was practising his profession when arrested.' The account ended by saying 'The refusal of the Federal Government to grant him the trial he demanded and then allowing him an unconditional pardon are proofs that they had no evidence to criminate him.'

After what must have been a very necessary and pleasant holiday John Clibbon returned to Savannah, Georgia, to recommence making his living as an artist. His mother, however, stayed on at Longueuil and, indeed, died there peacefully in her eighty-fourth year, in 1892.

Back in the South again our somewhat battered sailor tried to settle down to the humdrum routine of making a peacetime living. But his years in the worst sort of damp unheated prison cell had not helped. Some of the old sparkle had gone and his old wound was troubling him. Besides this we know from articles written in the *Confederate Veteran* twenty-seven years later that his fear of being permanently lame or partially crippled by rheumatism engendered of prison conditions had been realised. He was lame and in poor health until he died.

There seem to have been a number of contributory factors. He had been released, you remember, on a wave of public sympathy and newspaper publicity as the victim of politicians and the 'last of the Confederate naval personnel to suffer for having been successful'. This led to an embarrassing number of invitations, especially from bodies such as the 'Daughters of the Confederacy' —who conceded nothing in bellicosity to the militant 'Daughters of the Revolution'—to address meetings and sponsor Southern rehabilitation societies.

Reading between the lines, I am afraid these opportunities were not only unsettling but far too tempting in the possibilities they offered for 'fiddling expenses'—a practice not unknown in the business world but, as carried out by 'the master', done with the utmost delicacy and charm so that he left the society or township with the conviction that he had done them a thundering good turn. After all, I can almost hear him saying to himself, 'Well, it's only a refinement of the old post-war circus!' True, the humour had to be a little less robust for the wealthy wives of industrial promoters from the North or the railroad magnates of Tennessee or the cattle kings of Kansas and Nebraska. But the idea was the same and there was no longer any need to pass the hat round at the end of the performance—the splendid, indefatigable Daughters of the Confederacy did it for him!

Anyway, I imagine he graciously accepted a fee and certain expenses; the labourer was worthy of his hire. It was only in later years when the euphoria wore off and living became difficult with his physical disabilities that, as the newspapers hinted, many of the 'lectures' were self-promoted.

Brain was undoubtedly a good speaker, an amusing raconteur and, with his warm personality, a pleasant companion. He had had, after all, a not entirely uneventful time during the first nine years of his working life. But I would hazard a guess that a great number of these requests were the result of a kind of mass public conscience trying to make amends in arrears for what appeared to be a rather conspicuous blot on the sensitive American conception of state justice. It was not that the Puritanical commercialism of the North was developing any sort of conscience over plunder of the South, but it was nice, for politicians and businessmen alike, to appear to make amends in the comfortable shadow of the Bill of Rights without any awkward questions being asked.

A favourite cause was, of course, the erection of a monument to ex-President Jefferson Davis, who, in spite of a still-vocal minority of extremists in the Senate, had been set free as a symbol of goodwill. Like all good unemployed politicians and generals, he was writing his memoirs. But who was better qualified to tweak the heartstrings and loosen the purses of, this time, Texan ranchers and their families, than the only ex-Confederate naval officer still in the public eye? In fact, one of the last documents I have is the original billing of the Ragsdale's Opera House in Jacksonville, Texas. (see opposite).

I expect you, like me, will smile at the typical J.C.B. touch which is still there in the phrase 'with many amusing incidents'. Nor, if you remember the somewhat 'original' sea shanties of the circus, will you be surprised to hear that musical interludes continued to be a feature even of his lecture tours. We read in the *Confederate Veteran* (Vol. IV for 1896) that he was still going strong thirty years after the war. At the end of a long leading article entitled, 'Who is Commander J. C. Brain?' We learn,

> Another letter states that an old, scarred Confederate Veteran went to Austin, Texas and advertised for young ladies to accompany him on a tour through the States, to sing at his lectures. He claimed to represent the Jefferson Davis monument association. One lady worked for weeks for the success of the entertainment but it rained throughout.

What a pity; well, the rain falls, as the good book says, upon the just and upon the unjust with complete impartiality. And, between volumes IV and VI (1898) of the same magazine we learn that **Brain** had again been upsetting publishers by collecting pre-

Ragsdale's Opera House.

JACKSONVILLE, TEXAS,

Saturday Evening, Jan. 18th,

AT 7:30 O'CLOCK.

BENEFIT OF THE

Jefferson = Davis
MONUMENT.

COMMANDER

John C. Brain,

Formerly of the C. S. Navy,

The Last Prisoner of the War,

Will Deliver his Famous and Interesting

LECTURE

ON THE FOLLOWING SUBJECTS:

The Capture of S. S. "Chesapeake," out of New York Harbor, Dec. 5, 1863.

Capture of U. S. M. S. S. "Roanoke," off the Island of Cuba, Sept. 29, 1864.

Last Confederate Naval Expedition, which left Richmond, Va., Feb. 27, 1865, under orders for San Francisco, Cal.

The Capture of St. Mary's off Pautexen River Chesapeake Bay, April 1, 1865; cruise of the vessel and her destruction off the Island of Jamaica, June 19, 1865. With many amusing incidents.

Collection will be taken up for the benefit of the Jefferson Davis Monument Fund.

All the proceeds of these Lectures are forwarded to the Jefferson Davis Monument Association, at Richmond, Va.

Banner Steam Print, Jacksonville, Texas.

Original poster advertising
Brain's lecture at Ragsdale's
Opera House, Jacksonville

publication advances on his own initiative. What particularly roused their journalistic wrath and caused a flood of quite in-accurate vituperation was, of course, the sudden realisation that the 'Commander' in an impish mood had been pulling their legs and blissfully selling copies and subscription blanks of the very numbers which contained scathing articles on him and his doings. With a quiet smile he pocketed the money and called it all square.

He had been living between tours in Mobile, Alabama, and presumably had been making a little money at his father's old trade of illustrator and painter, but he decided to move again—perhaps it had become necessary. Even his regular pension, paid, not by the U.S. Government for wrongful imprisonment, but by the State of Tennessee on whose pension roll he had so far been, was stopped; because, it was explained, 'his demerits were shown'. Apparently, unlike a Mr. Sam Davis who is featured in the follow-ing paragraph, he had not 'caused the bosom of every Confederate to swell with supreme pride and a determination to raise a monu-ment'.

And so these last few years draw to a rather sad close. Brain is now in his sixties, tired and failing in health: the old sparkle has gone and he is alone. His two daughters, perhaps not unnaturally, are careful not to know him any more. They have disappeared not only from his life but from the family ken.

The last condescending little note on 'Commander' Brain comes from Sherman, Texas. After recalling that he was 'supposed to have captured a few ships', the correspondent said, 'Brain was lame, had a long and prominent scar on his left forehead . . . This battle scarred veteran (?) excited the sympathy of Confederates and was treated with due courtesy wherever he went. In some places his lecture proposition was not encouraged and he passed on to other towns.'

In two years the nineteenth century was to 'pass on'—to the honking of 500,000 new automobiles a year, 'you press the button, we do the rest' from Kodak cameras, and a 'ripple of satisfaction' from the *New York Times* at this 'year of wonders in business and production'.

In the midst of this bustle of opportunity and easy money we get a stark little sentence in the *Pictorial History of the Civil War*: 'He [John Clibbon Brain] died penniless in Tampa, Florida, in 1906.' No comment, no valediction recalling his years of useful endeavour, no kindly word of parting. The friends who once sang his praises in taverns during the last grim days of struggle were also long since dead. Perhaps he would have liked it that way; he had too much respect for time to waste it on self-pity.

Most Civil War historians, tempted perhaps by the contemporary newspapers, seem to have been so blinded by Brain the sower of wild oats that they almost missed not only Brain the sailor but even Brain the man. We are both historians by trade, but I must admit that we find him an intriguing and quite fascinating character; all the more so, perhaps, because of his completely amoral private life, and the sharp contrast this makes with his success as a privateer, which is after all what this book is about. He went to pieces in his old age, but that is a risk we must all take.

I cannot resist one whimsical thought. If his body lies in one of those Civil War cemeteries where the white headstones march in serried ranks, exactly spaced across the green hills beyond the regulation cherry trees, it will certainly be his last and only acceptance of military precision.

How shall we take our leave? Opportunist and showman, or successful sailor who would have been several times decorated in any normal war? You may take your choice.

His undoubted popularity with the common people of the village greens and the country inns, partly explains why he has received less than justice from the official documents, even in the South: documents which were compiled and presented by regular, professional naval officers. When they transferred their allegiance from the North at the outbreak of the war, they brought with them not only their substantive ranks but also a tradition of rigid behaviour and naval discipline, with its deep-seated horror of the unorthodox and the unconventional. Most of the other privateer captains were drawn from the ranks of the professional sailors; and, what is sometimes forgotten, they all had their ships provided for them, either built in England and smuggled out on some pretext, or seized in Southern ports at the commencement of hostilities. Brain had to acquire his the hard way, by going out into the enemy seas, dominated by the large and efficient U.S. Navy to capture them for himself.

When one looks back dispassionately over the years, his was no mean achievement for a young man of twenty-six; especially when one remembers that the bulk of such navy as the Confederate States managed to build or acquire remained bottled up in either the James River or the Mississippi during the whole of the war. He may have failed to get the *Roanoke* back to Wilmington for the mounting of guns and fitting out as a commerce raider, but much of the eleventh hour failure, was due to rank bad luck and not to lack of initiative or any shortage of animal courage. The *Chesapeake* loss was not his fault. He was ordered to hand over command and did so, to his credit, instead of sailing her into Wilmington direct.

In the end the acid test is, what damage did he inflict on the enemy? On any basis of calculation, this was considerable. If you examine the destruction caused by all the Confederate privateers, including those who had new fast ships built for them in England and armed with the latest guns by the Confederate agent in the U.K., Captain Bullock, you will find that only five—the *Alabama*, the *Florida*, the *Shenandoah*, the *Sumter*, and the *Tallahassee* sank a greater tonnage of shipping or caused as much chaos for the U.S. authorities as Brain did.

To sum up:

1. Brain's officially confirmed captures include:
   2 fast, ocean-going steamships
   2 large sea-going schooners
   3 brigs
   1 coastal vessel on passage (type unknown)
   1 yawl
   1 small Great Lakes steamer.
2. No record has come to light of:
   (a) Vessels destroyed during the week Brain operated on Lake Erie
   (b) Vessels captured by the *St. Mary's* between 2 April and 10 May 1865 (or whenever news of the capture of President Jefferson Davis actually reached the West Indies).

3. Three times Brain kept a considerable number of expensive cruisers looking for him quite unprofitably in the Atlantic when they were needed elsewhere to catch blockade runners.

4. He upset U.S. public morale quite badly on two occasions and nearly caused an international incident between the United States and Great Britain.

5. The boost to morale among the Southern forces, when, towards the end, all other news was of defeats, must have been out of all proportion to the material gains.

In a service much more rigidly tied to tradition than the army, which was largely amateur, his methods horrified senior professional naval officers. But curiously enough, in an ironic backhanded sort of way, he was a credit to that tradition itself. Any military system which can produce young officers who will return to the fight and take the personal risks he took, long after any hope of victory or reward had vanished, must have been a pretty good one.

What matter if in later years he bathed a little too obviously in the warm artificial glow of opera house platforms and popular ballads, printed by provincial papers and sung in taverns where men met to forget the more tedious affairs of the day? There are some who would say that he and other survivors had earned the right to do so.

When we look back on any war that has passed into history, we tend to remember the old men on the benches whom we knew, and to forget the young men on the march whom we can only guess at.

However that may be, and whatever conclusion you have come to during the course of these pages, I cannot help having a fleeting notion that, somewhere in those dark unknown silences beyond the moment of death, John Clibbon Brain, sometime commander in the naval forces of the Confederate States of America, will have managed to find a not inappropriate niche for his restless spirit.

Appendix

'The Ship's Bread is Very Queer Stuff'

AN EMIGRANT BRIG CROSSES THE ATLANTIC

For nineteenth-century emigrants, the passage across the Atlantic must have been something of an ordeal—uncomfortable, boring, and sometimes frightening, particularly for the majority who had little money and had to travel steerage. If the Brains bothered to send home any account of their own experiences—which I doubt —it has disappeared, but we are lucky enough to have the contemporary diary of a third emigrant from the family, J. C. Tabram's youngest son, Augustus Tomkins, who went across from Liverpool on the *Tuscarora* in 1849 when he was only twenty-one. His boyish diary, scribbled in pencil day by day, gives a better insight into conditions on an emigrant sailing brig of the mid-nineteenth century than any well-phrased history book or later journalistic reconstruction. Augustus was booked steerage but as soon as he saw the *Tuscarora* he wrote, 'Was most disappointed in position of the steerage and paid a pound more for a berth in the 2nd Cabin.' The next day he went aboard with what sounds like a mountain of luggage, including a sack of provisions and the evening after that they were ready to sail. The diary reads:

Oct. 13. Got into the river at 9 pm, was pleased with the sight of the opposite bank of the river; the lights are very pretty; smoked a pipe, had a drop of rum and water and went to bed.
Oct. 14. Weighed anchor and passed muster then got below and had some rum and water and bread and butter for breakfast: lots of people sick when the ship began to make sail— felt very giddy; was pleased with the appearance of the foam at the bow of the vessel. Saw the last of England, played a tune

on my flute to the sick people. [I simply dare not trust myself to comment.]

For the next four days most of the passengers were seasick and spent most of the time in their berths though Augustus did crawl up on deck at sundown on 15th to see the last of the Irish coast and make friends with an American from Philadelphia. A typical entry:

Oct. 18. Very rough, people ill all about—feel very queer; tried to cook some beef, burnt the saucepan and boiled the water out.

Then he got his sea legs.

Oct. 19. Turned out at 8 o'clock; going at eight and a half knots; bargained with the cook to do my grub; had ham and potatoes boiled with peas, onions and parsnips for dinner: a very rough night.

Oct. 20. Had a ducking on the weather bow of the vessel by a wave. Thanks to my feather pillow I sleep very well at nights; somehow or other I sleep while the rest are awake and complaining of the rolling of the vessel.

Oct. 21. Put on a clean shirt this morning, had cocoa (thanks to my friend Harry Coutts) for breakfast, with biscuit and jam. This is a beautiful morning, even on the sea there seems to be a difference between the day which God has set apart for his children to worship him and the six days of business. Went down to my cabin in the morning and read a few psalms and chapters; went to a prayer meeting in the Fore Cabin and gave out two hymns. Was annoyed with the disgusting language (in the presence of females and children) of my fellow passengers.

Oct. 22. Bacon and baked potatoes for dinner . . . A very pleasant night, smoked and sung on deck in the moonlight. Saw the Northern lights.

Oct. 23rd. Had biscuit and cocoa for breakfast; some of my beef for dinner which was first rate; saw a whale several times in the afternoon; in the evening a woman played several tunes very nicely on a tin whistle—some of the passengers danced, I stood by; afterwards singing on deck and in the fore cabin, was pressed to join in but would not, smoked a pipe on deck and enjoyed it.

Oct. 24. Biscuit with tea for breakfast; quite stormy today; had an allowance, together with a friend, of American pork (salted) for each person; had some of it for dinner (pretty good but rather too fat for me). Had some of my pickles after dinner they certainly are very nice—capital.

Oct. 25. Some coffee and biscuit and butter with sugar on it is a fine relish to me now . . . Very vexed this afternoon having lost my only coin, a sovereign; had a good hunt for it under the berths and shifted the boxes—but no go. I can't help it, but the worst of it is there are those in this cabin (I believe) think I have not lost it.

Oct. 28. Got up at eleven this morning; read Bible and *Life in Earnest*; very calm, potatoes and boiled bacon for breakfast; oatmeal cake for tea with sugar and butter. Went to the prayer meeting in the fore cabin. The first mate was overlooking the bending on of a foresail when a sailor carelessly threw a block down on deck without calling out to those below; the block struck the mate between the eyes and knocked him down, breaking the bridge of his nose. The first mate is misliked by most of the sailors.

Oct. 29. Had one of my beef bones cooked with a piece of beet, a carrot, turnip, parsnip, potatoes, onion cut up—a capital dinner and no mistake. Very rough; had a narrow escape, being pitched down the main hatchway through the ship rolling so much. I turned in early. The sea ran as high as the foreyard.

Oct. 30. Marmalade and biscuit for breakfast with some cakes out of my flour and jam, very nice; sold one shilling's worth of tobacco and two cigars; cakes of butter and flour for tea; an onion and biscuit and cheese, with a drop of brandy before going to bed; saw a lot of porpoises in the afternoon; ship going along in good style; gave my marmalade to a woman who is unwell—half a bottle.

Oct. 31. Biscuits getting low (The ship's bread is very queer stuff, have tried several times to eat it but cannot get on with it at all; it is as hard as a brick with a very disagreeable musty taste.) The Capt. ordered all the steerage passengers on deck to let the fresh air get through their clothes. He won't let them come aft because they are so filthy. Saw a sail bound for England. Very nice weather. Lots of dancing on deck in the moonlight, but it being just over my berth it was not very pleasing. Pickles before going to bed.

Nov. 1. Oatmeal porage for breakfast with cocoa; swabbed the deck belonging to our cabin. Had a bother with an Irishman; a great consternation on board caused by the flaming of the lamp while cleaning the vessel below. The Irish ran up screaming 'fire' and running about in all directions. It was extinguished directly.

Nov. 2. Porage for breakfast; biscuit, cheese and onion for dinner, a cake of flour and lard for tea. The weather is very foggy; it makes my clothes as damp as fine rain—the sailors tell me we shall have just such weather until we have passed the Banks of Newfoundland. We have had a good deal of sail up this last three days but have been going very slowly. Some very good singing on the deck last night.

Nov. 3. Read part of N. Thier's *History of the French Revolution*; had the other beef bone in some soup; read *Hearts and Houses* to Mrs. Ellis.

Nov. 4. (Sunday) Put on a clean shirt and stockings this morning; picked the beef bone cooked yesterday; went to the prayer meeting—just touched on the subject of the Church and Dissent with my mates, but knocked off fearing it would become too warm.

Nov. 5. Blew a stiff gale. A leak was reported to have made its appearance in the steerage, which created some alarm amongst the passengers. About ten o'clock the storm increased, the ship rolled very much. We were all in bed, a pot of putrid beef was upset which caused one of the most dreadful stinks ever smelt; just as we were crying out what could this be, the water, which was washing over the deck at the time came rushing in at the cabin windows. There was a general shout to those whose berths were under the lights, and the next we were all having a jolly laugh at them standing in their shirts with their beds and bedclothes on their backs. However they got another berth and

after a laugh at them in their new position the inhabitants of
the cabin ceased to articulate.

Nov. 6. We almost ran into a brig—the lookout did not see her
until we were close on her; the sea looked very beautiful
tonight—the tips of the waves look like sheets of fire.

Nov. 7. Had a fine breakfast this morning of hot cakes and
butter; dinner of ship's pork and potatoes baked in a tin. It
was very good; cake for tea. Cigar on deck with the Yankee.

Nov. 8. A corpse of a child was thrown overboard this morning. The Captain said something . . . and the ceremony was
concluded. A fair wind; read *Hearts and Houses*; smoked a clay
pipe after dinner.

Nov. 10. A woman died this evening in the steerage.

Nov. 11. The corpse was thrown overboard at half past four
this morning . . . Read *Life in Earnest*; beef cold for dinner with
vinegar and pickles. The sailors caught an owl in the rigging.

Nov. 12. Several birds in the rigging this morning; all were
captured . . . Caught a cold.

Nov. 13. Saw two vessels to the south—a pretty sight. Had a
cigar on deck with the Yankee; a fine night.

Nov. 14. Breakfasted at 7 o'clock on hot cakes and coffee; a
splendid day but tacking the ship every four hours.

Nov. 15. The wind changed into a favourable quarter early this
morning—going about ten knots . . . expect to see land this
evening; went very well indeed till about 8 o'clock when the
captain slackened sail for a pilot—until about half past twelve
when the vessel ran aground on Cape Henlopen; it was rather
awful, the ship kept thumping and digging into the sand in a
most uncomfortable manner.

The detailed account of this incident is too long to include here
but I cannot help just noticing the last two entries in this diary.
The first is obviously a rather hopeful, if not pathetic, attempt to
work out some sort of application, when he got ashore, in the
local newspaper for a job. It is crossed out a number of times and
much corrected. It reads:

In reply to an advertisement in the Ledger of today for a

journeyman printer, the subscriber would state that he under-
stands the general printing business—has worked at presses and
case in both job and newspaper houses and would be happy to
take a situation in the country, including satisfactory references.
A. T. Tabram.

There is something so simple and appealing, and we all remember
the first awful moments of trying to word either our first application for a job or our first reply to an advertised job.

The next little page is probably the last thing he ever wrote. It
is simply headed 'November 20th' and he was probably trying to
find somewhere in a strange country to lay his head. It reads:

Canvassed a great number of houses. Found that people have
been much put upon by canvassers. Very cold weather and
miserable walking. I have scarcely had a dry foot since I came
in the town. The people are moving in all directions. By now
it is snowing. The wind is very bleak.

He died a few days later and this diary and his rather pathetic
little bundle of belongings were sent back to my great-grandfather
(his father). The young Tabram children filled up the rest of the
little book with drawings and childish scribbles.

At the beginning of the diary there is an enchanting list of the
stores Augustus packed away in his sack for a month's living in
the steerage on an emigrant boat:

5 lbs rice	5 lbs sugar
$\frac{1}{2}$ lb tea	1 lb coffee
2 lbs cheese	1 lb tobacco
1 pint vinegar	2 quarts peas
flour	biscuit
bread	potatoes
apples	meat
bacon	polonies
herrings	onions
butter	treacle
pickles	pepper and salt

horseradish
brandy
parsnip
cocoa
ginger
turnips
cigars

lemons
carrots
marmalade
jam
mustard
tongue

On these he apparently lived happily for the month or five weeks of the voyage. He also took a box of books, and you may like to compare them to the sort of thing that you might take on a voyage these days! It was a most wonderful collection which included:

Dictionary of Knowledge
Johnson's Dictionary
Young Man From Home
Isaac's Poems
Two Bibles and a Hymn Book
A Poetical Companion
Tune Book
Gospel Witnesses
June's Pastoral

Tour in United States
Reference Book
Concordance
Eliza Cook
Jobbing Book
Printer's Guide
Elijah
Life in Earnest
Campbell's Life

Notes

1. The official historians of the naval side of the American Civil War were both men who had served in it personally. On the Federal side D. D. Porter finished the war as an admiral; on the Confederate side J. T. Scharf, though only a midshipman third class, junior, had seen a fair amount of active service. What is more important, however, is that both knew most of the leading figures in their navy personally, as well as having access to all records. One of the most valuable aspects of both histories is the number of reports and eye-witness accounts they include from the officers most directly involved. Neither Porter nor Scharf, incidentally, can be described as a completely impartial historian.

2. The family papers contain a mixture of letters, diaries, memoranda, and press cuttings. The written evidence has been supplemented by stories and anecdotes recounted by two aunts who knew Brain personally. These aunts were born in 1853 and 1860 and did not die until 1938 and 1943.

3. The teaset and the salt glaze bear are still in my possession.

4. Captain John Wilkinson was a regular naval officer who had a most distinguished career in the Confederate States Navy, particularly in command of one of the most successful blockade runners, the *R. E. Lee*. His *Diary of a Blockade Runner*, from which several quotations have been given, is therefore an important first-hand account of this aspect of the naval war. It is an enthralling book which gives a vivid picture of the dangers and excitements without, so far as one can judge, a word of exaggeration.

5. Raphael Semmes, another regular naval officer, started the war as a commander and finished as an admiral in the C.S.N. As early as April 1861 he was appointed to the command of the first Confederate privateer, the *Sumter*, then at New Orleans. He succeeded in getting her through the Mississippi blockade and captured eighteen ships in West Indian, South Atlantic, and European waters before being blockaded in Gibraltar by three Federal

cruisers. Semmes sold the *Sumter* and was appointed to the command of the ship that was to become the most famous of the Confederate privateers, the *Alabama*, with sixty-eight captures in twenty-two months in cruises extending from the Newfoundland Banks to the China Sea. Eventually the Federal cruiser *Kearsage* caught up with her when she had put into Cherbourg for fuel and repairs. Semmes came out to fight and the resulting battle is one of the legends of the Civil War. What he did not know was that the *Kearsage* was practically an ironclad and the result was a foregone conclusion.

6. The *Florida* and the *Alabama* were both built in England under contract with the Confederate naval agent, Captain J. D. Bullock. The purchase of unarmed merchant ships from a neutral power was perfectly legal under international law, so these ships were sailed out without guns or equipment and fitted out abroad, the *Florida* at Nassau and the *Alabama* at Terceira in the Azores. The U.S. authorities of course knew perfectly well the use to which these boats would be put and at times, when they had managed to obtain a court injunction to prevent the boats leaving England, a hurried and secret departure was necessary.

7. John Maffitt was yet another regular officer who made his mark as captain of a privateer, the *Florida*. Like Semmes he ran through the enemy blockade, in this case to get both into and out of Mobile. He had a long list of successes.

8. The attack on the *Chesapeake* was on 7 December 1863. The first mention in the *New York Times* was on 10 December, but then news filtered through so slowly that it was four days before the report of the next incident appeared. By 18 December, when the capture early the preceding day could be reported, the *Chesapeake* and Brain had become front page news.

9. Admiral Porter's description of these English-built blockade runners is interesting:

> Starting a hare with a pack of hounds would not create a greater excitement than when a long, lean, English-built steamer, with a speed of 16 knots an hour, suddenly found herself almost in the grips of the blockaders . . . To look at the beautiful lines of one of these small steamers (which often carried cargoes worth half a million) as she skimmed over the water, it would seem impossible that our improvised cruisers could overtake her. These vessels, built in England with all the science known to English

ship-builders, were sent fearlessly upon our coast, with a certainty that nothing we had could overtake them.

10. Even the biassed Admiral Porter admitted that the English had some good reasons for joining in blockade running. 'The Confederacy,' he wrote, was 'kept afloat by our cousins across the water, not so much from sympathy with the Southern people as from a desire to obtain cotton, which was so necessary for them to have to keep their mills going and prevent a revolt of the factory operatives'.

11. A short description of blockade duty from the other side might be of interest. It was written by Captain John Downes, engaged in the blockade of Charleston.

> I would be glad if I could only impress upon you some faint notion of how disgusting it is to us, after going through the anxieties of riding out a black, rainy, windy night in 3 or 3½ fathoms water, with our senses all on the alert for sound of paddles or sight of miscreant violator of our blockade and destroyer of our peace, when morning comes to behold him lying there placidly inside of Fort Sumter, as if his getting there was the most natural thing in the world and the easiest.

12. Wilkes was an officer with a knack of putting his foot into things. In November 1861 he had got near to bringing England into the war on the Confederate side by stopping an English ship and taking prisoner from her Mr. John Slidell and Mr. James Mason, Confederate commissioners to the courts of England and France. The British reacted to this insult to their flag by sending troops to Canada and it was only the timely release of the prisoners (after Wilkes had been regarded as a national hero for capturing them) that calmed down the situation. At this particular point Wilkes was also in trouble with his own authorities for unauthorised additions to his squadron of ships which had called in at Bermuda for other purposes.

13. Copies of the broadsheets of the 'Song of the *Roanoke*' and 'Three Cheers for Bold Brain' are among the family papers. Presumably Brain himself sent copies over to England—any covering note has been lost.

14. The naval Commander-in-Chief, Admiral Porter (the official historian) had had a varied war career comprising blockade duty, the river war on the Mississippi including the capture

of New Orleans, and the Red River campaign. He was appointed to the command of the North Atlantic squadron in preparation for the attack on Wilmington—a combined operation in which the Federal army and navy were at loggerheads from the first assault. Porter's history leaves no doubt that in his opinion the blame should be placed entirely on General Butler and success was indeed only achieved when General Terry took over command of the land forces.

15. The *Shenandoah*, another English ship, was especially equipped for an attack on the U.S. whaling fleet. Sailing from Las Desertas, an uninhabited island near Madeira where she had been armed and fitted out on 25 January 1865, she collected several prizes on the way to Australia where she went into dock for repairs. She then set out for the whalers in the north, where she created havoc, capturing thirty-eight ships in all. In her final attack on June 28 she collected and burned no fewer than eight. Captain Waddell finally heard that the war was over on 2 August when he met the British bark *Baracouta* off the Californian coast. He promptly dismounted his guns, closed his ports, whitewashed the funnels and disguised the *Shenandoah* as an ordinary merchantman. He then set sail for England and achieved the long voyage without communicating with another ship; he arrived at Liverpool on 6 November. There he turned his ship over to the British authorities who would have nothing to do with any attempt by the U.S. authorities to arrest him on charges of piracy.

16. Official Records of the Union and Confederate Navies, Series I, Vol. 5. For a list of main letters and despatches, see 'Sources and Bibliography', page 173.

17. Scharf's *History of the Confederate Navy*: when comparing accounts of events and operations in these two volumes with official British and United States documents or with reputable newspapers, we have been forced to the conclusion on a number of occasions that the accounts, collected from survivors by Scharf and published twenty-two years after the war, are in error. Furthermore, on several occasions, the accounts in Scharf contradict one another. The most notable of these, in the pages referring to Brain, are: (i) the *St. Mary's*—we have adhered to official British and United States archives accounts where necessary; (ii) the authenticity of Lieutenant Brain's papers in relation to the *Chesapeake*. Scharf attributed them to Parker, whereas Mallory, Secretary of State for the Navy, Admiral Semmes, commanding the Confederate naval forces, Dr. Jones, auditor, and Captain Maffitt of the *Florida* all

signed affidavits as to their authenticity. In any case, if there had been a detectable flaw in them, both the Canadian courts and the post-war United States courts would have been only too eager to prefer charges instead of having to admit there was no case to answer.

Sources and Bibliography

PRIMARY SOURCES

1. Private letters and diaries in the Tabram family papers.
2. Official letters and despatches from:
Official Records of the Union and Confederate Navies, Series I.
Public Record Office, London.
Jamaica Archives.
The most important of these are:
Despatch from Lt. Commander Wells of the *Galena* to Commodore
Foxhall Parker, commanding the Potomac Flotilla, April 4th, 1865.
Letter from the US Consul at Nassau to Acting Rear-Admiral Strib-
ling, US Navy, April 22nd, 1865.
Letter from the Resident, Turks and Caicos Islands to the Governor of
Jamaica enclosing a statement by the master of the schooner Charles
Turmell of Nassau, May 17th, 1865.
Report from Commodore Cracroft of the *Aboukir* to Governor Eyre
of Jamaica, June 12th, 1865.
Despatches from the Governor of Jamaica to the Secretary of State,
June 14th, 1865, and August 12th, 1865.
Instruction from the Principal Officer of Customs, July 14th, 1865.
Report from the Principal Officer of Customs to the Governor's
Secretary, December 5th, 1865.
3. Contemporary newspapers and magazines:
*The Times; New York Times; New York Daily Tribune; Free Press of
London* (Canada); *Halifax Gazette; Montreal Commercial Advertiser;
Quebec Mercury; Bahama Herald; Louisville Courier-Journal* (Kentucky);
The Confederate Veteran; Harper's Magazine, Jamaica Gleaner and Star.
4. Histories written by men who had taken part in the Civil War:
Davis, Jefferson, *Rise and Fall of the Confederate Government*, D. Appleton
& Co., New York, 1881.
Mahan, A. T., *From Sail to Steam*, Harper & Bros., New York and
London, 1907.
Porter, D. D., *Naval History of the Civil War*, Sampson, Low, Searle &
Rivington, London, 1887.
Scharf, J. T., *History of the Confederate States Navy*, Rogers & Sherwood,
New York, 1887.
Wilkinson, John, *The Narrative of a Blockade Runner*, Shelden & Co.,
New York, 1887.

SECONDARY SOURCES

Bowen, Frank, *The Sea, vol. 4*, Halton & Truscott Smith, London.

Catton, Bruce, *America Goes to War*, Wesleyan University Press, Connecticut, 1958.

Hill, Jim Dan, *Sea Dogs of the Sixties*, University of Minnesota Press, 1935.

MacBridge, Robert, *Civil War Ironclads*, Chilton Books, Philadelphia and New York, 1962.

Maclay, Edgar Stanton, *History of the American Privateers*, Sampson, Low, Marston & Co., London, 1900.

Miller, William, *A History of the United States*, Dell Publishing Co., New York, 1958.

Pratt, Fletcher, *Civil War on Western Waters*, Henry Holt & Co., New York, 1956.

Robinson, W. M. Jr., *The Confederate Privateers*, Yale University Press, 1928.

Smith, Edward, *England and America after Independence*, Constable, 1900.

Spears, John R., *History of the United States Navy, Vol. IV*, Bickers & Son, London, 1893.

Stern, Philip Van Doren, *The Confederate Navy—a Pictorial History*, Doubleday & Co., New York, 1962.

Thompson, W. M., Stephens, W. and Swan, W., *The Yacht America*, Charles E. Lauriet, Boston, 1925.

West, Richard S. Jr., *Mr. Lincoln's Navy*, Longmans, Green & Co., 1957.

Index

Acquia Creek 22, 26
Alden, Commander James 18

Bahama Islands 90–2, 106–7
Ballads 1, 109, 118–19, 123, 169
Bannut Tree House, Nailsworth,
  Glos. 5–11, 24, 47, 109, 140
Barney, Lieut. Commander, 32,
  43
Benjamin, the Hon. Judah P.
  (Confederate Secretary of
  State) 118
Bermuda 59, 63, 66, 95, 106,
  110, 131
Bermuda Mirror 118
Blockade runners, blockade
  running 79–88, 169
Brain, Elizabeth 8–11, 76, 142,
  150
Brain, John 10–12
Brain, John Clibbon: early life
  5; arrival in America 12;
  notoriety 12–13; settlement in
  Virginia 16; enlistment 22;
  transfer to navy 24; posting
  to *Jamestown* 24; part in naval
  engagement in Hampton
  Roads 27–41; Secret Service
  work 43–7; promotion 45;
  capture of the *Chesapeake* 48–
  71; escape from Canadian
  authorities 71; activities
  round Lake Erie 72–5; visit

to his mother 76; gets to
  Nassau and Havana 77–92;
  capture and loss of the
  Roanoke 93–120; return to
  Virginia 121–2; ballads about,
  1, 109, 118–19, 123; capture
  of *St. Mary's* 125–8; last
  cruise to West Indies and
  destruction of *St. Mary's*
  128–39; settles in Georgia
  140; the circus 141;
  imprisoned 143–50; lecture
  tour 151–2; last years 154–7
Bristol State Militia 20
Brook, Lieut. John 30
Buchanan, Capt. 15–16, 31–2
Bullock, Capt. J. D. 97, 98,
  156, 168

Cape Fear River 82
Charlestown 48, 77, 92, 121,
  128, 142
Chatard, Capt. F. 43
Chesapeake, the 48–71, 128, 156;
  international argument about
  68–71
Chesapeake Bay/River 16, 27–
  41, 125, 129
Civil War, background to 14–19;
  description of 20–26;
  Confederate position in 1864
  77–9